Philosophy
and
Theology

PRAISE FOR
JOHN CAPUTO'S
PHILOSOPHY AND
THEOLOGY

"I meant to take a quick glance at Jack Caputo's new book but then couldn't put it down. It's rare for a theologian to be interesting, and rarer for a philosopher perhaps, but this book is full of intriguing insights expressed through sparkling prose—profound, delightful, and downright inspiring."
—Brian McLaren, author/activist
(anewkindofchristian.com)

"Imagine a book in which Augustine of Hippo and Jacques Derrida are co-cupids, each aiming their arrows at your heart. Only in the hands of Jack Caputo would this be imaginable. This is a lyrical, incredible, impossible gem of a book. Caputo sings, preaches, waxes philosophic and theologic, and ultimately brings us into the presence of two giants—Augustine and Derrida—each at prayer; what surprises us is that they're praying together. And, if we read carefully, we'll see that this little book is, in fact, Caputo's own prayer. I will read this volume many times."
—Tony Jones, national coordinator of Emergent-US
and author of The Sacred Way

"Here once again the author shows with typical brio, gusto, and caputo (to coin a phrase) that philosophy and theology are like two twins engaged in loving and creative combat. The style is crisp, the arguments concise, the conclusions lucid and arresting. This pioneering book is accessible to both academic and nonacademic readers alike. Passionate reading at its best."
—Richard Kearney, Boston College

"Elegant, clear, and provocative, John D. Caputo's *Philosophy and Theology* adds a new twist to a debate as old as the West itself. Still the father of the Philosophy of Religion, in its continental register in America, Caputo has also become its main gadfly."
—Kevin Hart, The University of Notre Dame

"In searching for a text introducing students into the rich dialogue between philosophy and theology, there is no better find than John Caputo's *Philosophy and Theology*. Several pages into Caputo's text, one realizes that we are receiving far more than an introduction. This concise and accessible text stands on its own as a primary text, revealing the wisdom and passion of a scholar who presses through traditional boundaries to new ends. While providing students a new way of thinking about the relationship between philosophy and theology, Caputo offers his own breathtaking theological meditation in the same line as the great thinkers that he engages."
—Shelly Rambo, Boston University

"*Philosophy and Theology* is a remarkable little essay, at the same time wide-ranging and deep, simple yet profound. It is beautifully written, witty, and compelling, recounting the changing relationship of theology and philosophy throughout history.... This gem of a book is a must read for every budding philosopher and theologian—indeed, for every practicing philosopher and theologian."
—James H. Olthuis, Professor Emeritus of Philosphical Theology, Institute for Christian Studies, Toronto

"By bringing to light the intimacy between the seemingly independent domains of philosophy and theology, Caputo dispels a still widely held belief that 'religious people have checked their rational faculties at the door.' With humor and verve, he tracks the history of their relation from its pre-modern expressions to the radical shifts imposed by the role of science in establishing new rules of thought. The Enlightenment may have provided a necessary corrective to the rationality that shored up religious narratives, but Caputo shows how postmodernity allows for the return of passion and prayer in human existence.... Numerous original works have established John D. Caputo as a significant original thinker and an interpreter of the philosophical tradition. The present book is indispensable for both those seeking entrée to and those already familiar with this terrain."
—Edith Wyschogrod,
J. Newton Rayzor Professor Emerita, Rice University

"Just as Socrates claimed 'the unexamined life is not worth living' so too, it may be said, that the unexamined theology may not be worth believing. In this brief but provocative work, Caputo urges both philosophers and theologians to re-examine their search for truth, meaning, and beauty, and in so doing, demonstrates why, now more than ever, both must be prepared to listen and learn from one another."
—Ronald P. Mahurin, Vice President,
Council for Christian Colleges and Universities

"What hath Nietzsche to do with Augustine? In this book, one of the most influential figures in continental philosophy of religion offers a provocative—and entertaining—postmodern rendition of the enduring question: What does Athens have to do with Jerusalem? Caputo provides an enlightening excursion through the history of philosophy and theology, all the while with an eye on our postmodern situation.... [H]is engaging proposal will provoke students to think long and hard about these perennial questions."
—James K. A. Smith, Calvin College

HORIZONS IN THEOLOGY

Philosophy and Theology

JOHN D. CAPUTO

Abingdon Press
Nashville

PHILOSOPHY AND THEOLOGY

Copyright © 2006 by Abingdon Press

This book is printed on acid-free paper.

Library of Congress Cataloging-in-Publication Data

Caputo, John D.
    Philosophy and theology / John D. Caputo.
        p. cm.
    ISBN 0-687-33126-9 (pbk. : alk. paper)
    1. Philosophy. 2. Theology. I. Title.

B29.C2745 2006
261.5'1—dc22

ISBN 13: 978-0-687-33126-0

2005030356

08 09 10 11 12 13 14 15—10 9 8 7 6 5 4

MANUFACTURED IN THE UNITED STATES OF AMERICA

CONTENTS

INTRODUCTION

In a passage that has always remained with me, the young Friedrich Nietzsche envisaged the following scene. Once upon a time, on a little star in a distant corner of the universe, clever little animals invented for themselves proud words, like truth and goodness. But soon enough the little star cooled, and the little animals had to die and with them their proud words. But the universe, never missing a step, drew another breath and moved on, dancing its cosmic dance across endless skies.

Has Nietzsche described our fate? Does anyone know we are here? Or care? Does a faith in God relieve us of the horror of this scene once and for all? Or is this scene inescapable, not because it can be firmly established as the final truth, but because it remains a possibility that haunts and menaces faith like a ghost? And in constantly menacing faith, does this eerie scene in fact help to constitute faith as faith, which does not see in whole but only in part?

That question, that cluster of questions, is for me the way the issues of philosophy and theology get raised, the two together. The two have always overlapped for me, intertwining and communicating with each other in kind of endless contest and collaboration that constitutes their history

1

across the centuries. The philosophers and the theologians go for the "ultimates," the deepest questions we ask ourselves, or better, that keep imposing themselves upon us. Philosophers and theologians are slightly unstable types, people who have been knocked off their pins by such questions, who have been drawn into an exploration of the outer and inner space of our lives. Each proceeds with a wary eye on the other, ranging over much the same territory—God and ethics, our origin and our destiny—sometimes jealously and combatively, sometimes cooperatively, conducting a kind of lover's quarrel over the ages.

ONE

I start these deliberations by defending the thesis that in the confrontation—both the contests and the collaborations—of "philosophy and theology," these two great titans of Western thought and culture, the most important word is the "and." That may seem like cowardice on my part, an unmanly attempt to sneak out the back door as the two great men come striding into the room. But here I stand. I can do no other. Everything depends on the "and." Sometimes "and" announces a happy coming together of two things belonging together, where the two seem to be meant or made for each other, as when the pastor says "I now pronounce you husband *and* wife." But sometimes it poses a challenge, gets in our face and stares us down and says, "I dare you to try to get those two together in the same room!" Then the title would sound more like saying "Democrats and Republicans" assembled to debate the federal budget. Then the "and" is sure to set off sparks and be the occasion of a fight, like the sort of "and" that you see if this couple ended up in divorce court. A lot of times when we say "and," it turns out we mean "against" or "versus," and we are trying to start a fight. When Larry King tells us he is having an outspoken liberal "and" an outspoken conservative on his show tomorrow night to discuss gay marriage, we all

3

tune in expecting a lot of outspeaking. The "and" may signify a happy marriage or an unhappy one, a wedding or a war, a quiet meditative dialogue of two old friends or a TV talk show shouting match. Should we counsel these two to go their separate ways and not even think about getting together?

So we have a lot on our plate. We need to get an idea not only of what philosophers and theologians do in their separate workshops but also, over and above this already tall order, to determine how they communicate with each other, which involves the tiny "and" that might otherwise have slipped our notice.

Why so much timidity? What has us worried is the built-in turf war between philosophers and theologians. While they raise overlapping questions about the ultimate meaning of our lives, they are coming from different directions. The theologians belong to communities of faith, and their work is to think through the "tenets of faith" or the "contents of revelation," both the words of the Scriptures and the common faith passed down by the faithful over the ages. We might even take that as a working definition of theology, that it is the place where the community of faith does its thinking, examining, clarifying, conceptualizing, and updating the common faith over the course of its history. That is why theologies—and there are many of them—come in different stripes. Some are conservative, more insular, bent on keeping as rigorously as possible to the sacred words and avoiding too much contamination by worldly ways of thinking like philosophy. Some are progressive, constantly rethinking the ancient faith in dialogue with the world, "correlating" it with the surrounding culture, especially with philosophy.[1]

The philosophers, however, like to think of themselves as a more independent lot, as freelancers, working on their own, not the delegates of any community of faith, with no one to report to but themselves, or so they say. Philosophy, the philosophers claim, is reason all the way down (to its foundations) or all the way up (to its first principles). Philosophers claim they are making arguments about the universal human situation, about the meaning and makeup of things in general, of their basic or ultimate "what" and "why" and that they do so without recourse to any external authority, solely based on sound logic and sound observation.

As you see, philosophy and theology make claim to much the same turf—both are interested in the questions of God and of the good life and of what being "human" means, for example—but in importantly different ways, which is why there is bound to be competition and conflict between them, along with the possibility of cooperation. Both have things to say about the Nietzschean riddle with which we began. Doing philosophy is a matter of being a keen observer and having a bit of a head for logic, the philosophers say, and anybody from San Francisco to Singapore is welcome to try it. Theology presupposes you have a particular religious tradition that you are trying to explicate—although the more progressive theologians want their theology to be as public and universal as possible, delivering a message to everyone. That is the usual way of rendering the difference between them, and one of the things we will be doing here is testing how well this common account actually holds up. For example, Western philosophers tend to say very Western things about death and individuality that are of interest mainly to Western people and that differ markedly from non-Western traditions. So are the philosophers deceiving themselves? Do they actually have a constituency that they do not realize they have? Do philosophers not always and inevitably end up serving as spokespersons for certain communities? By the same token, just as it is true that the theologians have churches to report to, to what extent do the philosophers have to report back to the universities in which they are nowadays housed, since they no longer walk about ancient forums conducting (tuition-free) discussions?

If we think of philosophical and theological thinking as two different *acts* or modes of thinking, as two different dimensions of a whole human life, then we can imagine the two acts cohabiting happily in the same head, yielding a person who would be a thinking believer, or a believing thinker, a person of learning and of faith. There are examples of that—of religious philosophers and philosophical theologians—as far as the eye can see. It happens all the time in religious communities with strong theological and philosophical traditions, with traditions that bring forth Christian intellectuals or Jewish intellectuals or Islamic intellectuals, just to name a few. That sort of thing has been going on for millennia. The history of religion is veritably studded with such people. As a matter of fact, it is only since the eighteenth century that atheism has gotten any kind of footing at all among Western intellectuals, although one has to admit that ever since then it has held a special attraction for many of them. But before that, everyone had a religious faith and the distinction between the philosophical and the theological was employed simply to mark off or allocate what one knows by "reason" and what one believes by "faith."[2]

But if we think that the distinction between philosophy and theology means there are two *types* of people out there, two different styles of life—a theological life of faith and the philosophical life of reason—then we are more likely to get a battle. Then the world gets divided into two types who seem forever at odds, those who are guided by faith in a power higher than themselves and are willing to put up with a certain amount of non-seeing, of seeing only "in part" and "through a glass, darkly," as Saint Paul says (1 Cor. 13:9-12 KJV), who take a kinder view of authority and tradition; and those who insist on seeing for themselves, who rely on their own powers and resources, who are suspicious of tradition and authority. It is easy to see the sort of names each will call the other. The theologians will think the philosophers are full of

6

themselves, that they are proud and vain, while the philosophers think that theologians are just a little batty and they are baffled by the things—like angels and demons!—that theologians let inside their heads.

This battle broke out right at the beginning of philosophy, where it first appeared as, in part, a way of getting beyond the old religious myths. Philosophers number Socrates among their patron saints, a secular saint, of course, not somebody who is up in heaven keeping watch over them. Socrates went about Athens asking questions of everyone high or low in search of the definition of the virtues. Socrates made no pretense to know the answers himself, but in the process Socrates made those who thought they knew the answers look bad when he showed them that they did not. As you can imagine, that choice of vocations turned out badly for Socrates, and the Athenians repaid him for all the embarrassment he caused them by executing him after a famous trial. The charges? He was corrupting the youth and was an atheist. Philosophers greatly admire and try to imitate Socrates— except for the bits about execution and accepting no pay for his teaching. They think part of the problem Socrates ran into was his brush with traditional religious beliefs. They take the trial of Socrates, and later on the trial of Galileo, as a warning that theology spells trouble for anyone who wants to think for himself and ask a lot of embarrassing questions. The word *theology* means for many philosophers a system of irrational and dogmatic beliefs that tolerates no dissent. Many a philosopher who doesn't agree with anything else the twentieth-century German philosopher Martin Heidegger says would agree with Heidegger that the idea of a "Christian philosophy"—this idea of a believing thinker or thinking believer— is a square circle. For Heidegger, if you are a believer, then you have decided to take an early retirement on thinking. You think you already have the answers to the sort of questions Socrates asked and you can't play the game, or perhaps better, what philosophy you do will be just that, just a game you are playing, because you have the real answers up your theological sleeve. You start with the answer and try to retrofit it with a proof that will get you where you wanted to go all along. That, by the way, is one thing that menaces the idea of relying on pure "arguments" or formal "proofs" and saying that you are following pure "reason." When you get to the hot-button issues in both philosophy and theology, where people have deeply held beliefs on "gut issues," people try to find proofs to back up their gut feeling rather than letting the chips of thinking fall where they may. (One of the marks of philosophy and theology, for better and for worse, is that the arguments go on and on. As one wag has put it, "philosophy" means "unanswerable questions," and "theology" means "unquestionable answers.")

However, Socrates is not without his admirers among the theologians. They agree that the "unexamined life is not worth living," just as Socrates said. They think that religious faith does not put questioning to sleep but, on the contrary, exposes the depths of our existence, releasing an endless chain of reflection and a lifelong search that starts out from a humble confession of how little we know. One of the things that theologians admire about Socrates, of which, they think, the philosophers might take a little more heed, is how deeply convinced Socrates was about his own ignorance and limitations and what a salutary warning he constitutes against the sin of pride. Many centuries after Socrates, Søren Kierkegaard would make it his life's work to be a "Christian Socrates." Kierkegaard thought his situation in nineteenth-century Denmark was singularly Socratic. He was in search of what it means to be a genuine Christian the way Socrates sought true virtue, and he thought that while the world around him considered itself Christian, the hard truth was that it was not, not if being Christian meant really following the New Testament and not just paying it lip service. So Kierkegaard took it as his task as a thinker to disabuse what he called "Christendom" of the illusion that it was in fact really "Christian"—he was not likely to be elected a bishop on a platform like that. He made no pretense to actually being a Christian himself and said that at best he was trying to become one. That, in fact, is what the word *philia* in "philosophy" means, a lover, someone wounded by Cupid's arrow, someone who conducts a loving search for wisdom. Kierkegaard was in that sense deeply Socratic, deeply *philo*sophical, in search of and trying to become a Christian, just the way Socrates was in search of wisdom. Both Kierkegaard and Socrates were philosophers, the difference between them lying in Kierkegaard's faith that wisdom is ultimately found only in Christ, while Socrates thought it was found in the form of life embedded in the Greek *polis*.[3] Those differences make all the difference, of course, and it does no good to underestimate them. But it is also important for us to see how they communicate with each other.

TWO

The second thesis that I will advance in this little essay, this one a little bolder—I am gathering my courage as I go along—is this: the tendency for a battle to break out between philosophy and theology is exacerbated in *modernity*. By modernity I mean very roughly the period from the seventeenth century (the origins of modern science) to the first half of the twentieth century, although the holes and gaps in that much too easy periodization are embarrassingly large. The tendency of modernity is to insist that reason—or shall we say Reason, since reason had great prestige in those days, enough to merit capitalization—can stand on its own two feet, that reason can think and do for itself. Reason is autonomous and has come of age, which means that in modernity things like "faith," "tradition," and "authority" come under fire. Dare to think for yourself (*sapere aude*) was its motto—dare to use your head, dare to grow up! If that makes the modern idea of reason sound like a teenager, that is not an accident. For Immanuel Kant—who invoked this motto in answering the question "What is Enlightenment?"—Enlightenment is intellectual maturity. Enlightenment (the main engine in modernity) means the day the West grew up, like an eighteen-year-old home from college for the first time telling his parents that while he will continue to accept their money, thank you very much, he may not always accept their advice, considering how antiquated and hidebound is their thinking. While modernity may be a modern phenomenon, that particular scene is not. The ancient Greek playwright Aristophanes wrote a comedy about it called *Clouds*, which is also a spoof of Socrates. You should look it up sometime, particularly if you are looking for arguments to make against your parents.

Regarding my second slightly stronger thesis, the climate for a happy marriage between philosophy and theology, the "and" in the positive sense was a lot better in the *pre-modern* world, before modern science and modern political tendencies changed the atmosphere. Speaking very broadly, in those times, sometimes called "the age of faith," theology was the premier and prestige discourse of the day, the way science is today. Theology was called the "queen of the sciences," and it tended to be the ultimate authority, the conversation stopper, just the way that today starting a sentence out by saying, "Science has shown . . ." tends to silence everyone else in the room. Whenever royalty speaks the rest of us are cowed.

So what you think about modernity lies at the root of many of the arguments you hear about philosophy and theology. Although I am going to say some sharp things against modernity, I am not about to advocate that we try somehow to reinstate the pre-modern order. While the pre-modern eludes many of modernity's failings, it also offends our "modern democratic" instincts. It was a time in which people were all willing to sign on to the idea that there is a deep hierarchical, top-down order inscribed in things, the heavens and God up above and earth and us down below—notice how these ideas of God are related to a pre-Copernican imagination—with kings and queens above and everyday ordinary people down below, priests up, laypeople down, men up, women down. And finally theology above and philosophy below, as a "handmaiden" to the queen. Now it is a sad but true point, almost an unbroken principle in human affairs, that whoever has the power abuses it, and if someone has absolute power he or she abuses it absolutely. The democratic solution the American founders came up with is that the best thing to do is to distribute the power among an optimal number of parties who exercise a system of checks and balances on one another and to make sure that nobody gets all the power, and nobody can say *"l'état, c'est moi,"* I am the state. The most they can say is that they were elected for a term of office and they are eventually expected to clear off their desk and go home when their term is up, as George Washington was the first to do. But however you work it out, whoever gets the power—in our case, whether it be philosophers or theologians—the other one, who lacks the power, is in trouble. In the age of faith—roughly the period that stretches from Saint Augustine to the High Middle Ages— theologians had the power, so there was tendency on their part to treat the philosophers roughly, as handmaidens (or worse) and to threaten anyone who dissented, especially the "philosophers," with the torch. Theologians sometimes used the word philosophy abusively, as an insult, meaning pagans, non-believers, just the way many philosophers today, when they want to insult something, call it theology, meaning dogmatic faith. That was definitely the downside of the pre-modern world, which is why I am not arguing to reinstate it.

But at its best, and this is the reason I am turning to it (without advocating returning to it), the great theologians of that period said some very interesting and sensible things about faith and reason, things that have today resurfaced and have acquired a surprising currency. They put faith in a particular light from which we today have something to learn. At the very end of these reflections, I will introduce a third possibility, the *postmodern*, where I will say that the pre-modern prefigures the postmodern in certain ways, that the two are interestingly interactive. I will argue that there is something basically right about giving faith this kind of play, although we obviously have to build a lot of precautions into that lest we be revisited by this top-down way of thinking. But what interests me about the pre-modern is the productive interplay between philosophy and theology we find there. All of the great doctrines of Christian theology, the Trinity and the Incarnation first among them, were worked out in the early centuries of the church in a close dialogue with Greek philosophy. Saint Paul had said that philosophy was foolishness, but Paul thought the world was about to end, and he absolutely could not foresee or even dream of the world that would take shape after Constantine became a Christian. Then Christian thinkers sat down to table with the wisdom of this world, a process that culminated in the towering achievement of Saint Augustine, whose long shadow stretches over the history of theology to this day, and through Augustine came pouring into Christianity and into Western culture, a stream of philosophical assumptions that Augustine inherited from Greek philosophers.

I will provide two examples of the way philosophy and theology worked together in the pre-modern world, and the differences between them are instructive. The first example, Saint Anselm, comes from the predominantly Augustinian direction, which means ultimately from Plato, while the second, Saint Thomas Aquinas, belongs to the thirteenth century, a time when Aristotle had become very important. So it already tells us a lot that in the Middle Ages the two broad streams of theology were marked off in advance by two Greek philosophers, Plato and Aristotle. If you want to see the difference between those two, find a reproduction of Raphael's *School of Athens*. Raphael portrays Plato with his right hand pointing skyward, meaning that the true world is above, of which this sensible world here below is a copy, which is congenial to one kind of theology. Aristotle, however, spreads his right hand out over the ground in front of him, which means that you always start with the sensible world under your nose, which is the keynote of another way to do theology. A good deal of the Reformation that Luther set off consisted in trying to run both these Greek philosophers off theology's premises, claiming that while they were both the work of the devil, Aristotle in particular was an especially devilish chap. But if you run the philosophers out of town, the result is inevitably to weaken theology, too, and you will reduce seminary training to Bible thumping and choir practice. Religion needs theology and theologians need philosophy if they are going to do anything more than tell us that God told them so when pressed about their faith. The great theologians of the Middle Ages understood the intimate relationship of philosophy and theology, that the one tends to provoke the other into rethinking assumptions and hence that they nourish each other. So it does no good for either one to call the other the work of the devil and to try to go it alone as if they alone spoke with the tongues of angels.

I have in mind Saint Anselm's famous "proof for the existence of God," which can be found in all the anthologies used in courses on the philosophy of religion. The philosophers have tagged this deeply theological meditation the "ontological argument," which means an effort to prove the existence of God from the very meaning of the idea *God*. By God, Anselm says, we can all agree that we mean a being than which no greater can be conceived. For God would not be God if there were something greater than God. But if something exists merely in our mind but not in reality, the thing that exists in reality is greater. So if God exists merely in our mind and not in reality, anything that really exists is greater than God, which is contrary to the idea of God. Therefore, God exists in reality and not merely in our mind.

Many very good philosophical theologians have found something fishy in this argument, even as a lot of very good ones support it. I am not about to be drawn into the black hole of analyzing its twists and turns, except to tell you, for your information, that I agree with its opponents. What interests me is not the objections to the proof itself, but the objection that it is to be read as a "proof" at all, a proof in the "modern" sense, in the sense of an argument that stands freely on its own two philosophical feet.

As both the Protestant theologian Karl Barth and the contemporary Catholic philosopher-theologian Jean-Luc Marion have argued, this purely modernist and philosophical take on the proof is a mistake. While Anselm was certainly offering an argument, the context in which Anselm does so makes it clear that the formal argument plays a completely supporting role in a larger drama, that Anselm is saying to his fellow monks—he was addressing monks, not the American Philosophical Association—that their religious life of prayer and personal sacrifice should be buoyed by the idea that God is a being of such perfection that God is just there, there by his very perfection, irrepressibly, overflowingly there. Anselm was trying to awaken in them the idea that God is first, last, and always; the alpha and the omega; above us and within us and around us; before us and after us; inside us and outside us; so much so that it is better to think not that God is in us as that we are in God. In other words, Anselm was formulating an idea of God that expressed his religious experience of living "through Him, and with Him, and in Him," as the ancient liturgical hymn says, and he did not think this a freestanding argument (= philosophy). In a sense he was saying this is not an argument (in the modern sense) but an effort at conceptualizing or clarifying something that is intuitively obvious to all those people who experience God in their daily lives. In fact, when Anselm said this, he wasn't standing, he was kneeling, and this bit of reasoning was meant to clarify the God of his faith, the God given to him in the life of prayer. If you examine the *Proslogian*, the text in which this argument is found, you will see that it begins with a prayer. I say that

Anselm's approach was broadly Augustinian and Platonic because he seeks for God above not by going outside but by going within. I sought You abroad, among the outer things of the world, Augustine said in the *Confessions,* when all along You were within me, which also means that he seeks for God by seeing that God has first sought us out.

Thomas Aquinas thought that Anselm's argument was not so much false as it was slightly precipitous. He agreed that the overwhelming being of God was intuitively obvious and crushingly clear—*if* you had an intuitive and direct knowledge of God. But, he thought, that is something waiting for us in eternity, while here on earth the only things whose existence is intuitively and directly given to us are the physical things in the world around us. Remember the pose struck by Aristotle in Raphael's painting—to which Aquinas appended Romans 1:20, that we know the invisible things of God from the visible things of this world. Aquinas thought that as a philosopher, and this was pretty much what he meant by philosophy, you start out with what is evident to our senses and reason up from there. You can get to God that way, but the God you get will be a pretty thin philosopher's God. Remember that in those days, they did not divide things up the way we do in modern college curricula and that philosophy meant the whole range of arts and sciences, or "secular knowledge," whatever is not law, medicine, or theology, which is why even today everybody gets a Ph.D., a doctor of philosophy. Theologians, however, start out with God and approach the world from the standpoint of God, although that does not mean that the idea of God has been planted in their souls from birth. It means that they start with what they accept as given in revelation and what they believe with the aid of grace, which contains a very thick and robust idea of God. Then they must do the best they can to clarify it by means of rational argument and conceptual analysis.

Aquinas considered himself a theologian, and he speaks as a man of Christian faith although he uses a lot of philosophy on the job. His major work, the one excerpted in all the medieval philosophy courses, is called the *Summa Theologiae*, a "summary of theology." However, when he said "the philosopher," he meant Aristotle. But one of the reasons that Aquinas became so famous is the delicate equilibrium he established between theology (reasoning down from faith) and philosophy (reasoning up from the senses)—but either way using reason. Philosophy could lead a considerable distance along the way until its powers faded and then theology took its hand from there and crowned its efforts. Grace perfects nature. As a Christian with an Aristotelian streak, Aquinas thought that our nature was wounded by sin but not that it was vitiated and corrupted all the way down and that we should fall back on faith in desperation. That particular idea broke out with a fury in the Reformation and it went back to Augustine, not to Aquinas. Aquinas thought that our senses and rational faculties were made by God and they were capable of working very well, as is anything God has made, but that as natural and human faculties they were limited and imperfect, and this imperfection is made up for by grace, thanks be to God. If you detract from the things God has made, he said once, you detract from the power of God. Aquinas combined the first creation story in Genesis, that what God made is good, indeed very good, with Aristotle's robust sense for the reality of the sensible world around us, in a kind of Christian realism. He did not think the world was a Platonic "copy" or "imitation" of real being. He thought that the world had its own proper, proportionate, and intrinsic reality, but that this reality, however robust, was a finite and limited edition of what God is infinitely and perfectly. That is also why Aquinas thought that the Christian faith in the Incarnation, where matter and bodily life is nothing lowly but worthy to be the scene of God's advent on earth, while a matter of revelation, makes a great deal of sense.

To give you a contemporary example of how Thomas
Aquinas viewed things, consider the current controversy
about *Intelligent Design*, which is the notion that the
makeup of the human body—the human eye is a good
example—is too complex to be explained by random selection,
and we must conclude that its evolutionary genesis was
immediately directed by an intelligent designer, like God.
Saint Aquinas said that God acts through "secondary
causes," that is, God does not do everything directly himself. God creates nature, nature has been given its laws, and
these laws in some way reflect God's being and glory. God
gives nature its own space (literally and figuratively!) and
lets natural processes unfold according to these laws. We
leave it to natural scientists to tell us precisely what in particular those natural laws are and, therefore, how God's
glory eventually is going to be revealed in them. Whatever
is good science is *ipso facto* good from God's point of view,
but we have to wait for the science to come in. God, like
any good executive, does not micromanage what God has
created, and we do not need theology monitoring biology's
or astronomy's every move. From Aquinas's point of view,
what is today called Intelligent Design would constitute a
series of miraculous (supernatural) interventions required
just to keep the natural world running, like a driver
constantly making micro-adjustments to the steering wheel
to keep an automobile in the right lane. Of course, Thomas
Aquinas does not deny miracles. He just does not think
that natural processes are kept on course by a series of
miracles. He reserves miracles for supernatural events—the
events described in the Scriptures, like the virgin birth or
the miracles of Jesus, etc.—not natural events, like the
movements of heavenly bodies or, if he had known about it,
the course taken by evolution. That is why the Catholic
Church, which takes Aquinas as its hero, has never gotten,
and should not get, hysterical about evolution. The church

went through all that with Galileo, when it made the embarrassing claim that theology commits us to thinking that the sun runs its course around the earth.

Of course, there is something a little unnerving about all this to the traditional, more Augustinian way of doing theology. Aquinas had a robust faith *both* in the grace of God *and* (there is our word again!) in the natural world or in natural processes generally. That made the more Augustinian traditionalists nervous, and some traditionalists today trace modern atheism back to Aquinas. They don't mean that Aquinas was an atheist, of course—the man was a Dominican friar and a saint. But they think Thomism (as in "Thomas" Aquinas) is a slippery slope at the end (or bottom) of which is naturalism, and they prefer to think of nature as somewhat more wounded and in need of help; that way God is less likely to appear as superfluous.

But on either approach, the Augustinian/Anselmian or Thomistic—politically that also represents a division between two major and competing religious orders, the Franciscans and Dominicans—there is no antagonism between theology and philosophy. The supernatural gift of faith seeks to understand itself in theology, and philosophical reason is the natural means, the natural gift, God has given us to do so. Theology is no more opposed to philosophy than the head is opposed to the feet; if they cooperate, we can eventually get most anywhere we choose. Faith seeks to understand what it believes (*fides quaerens intellectum*) and the understanding seeks to know what can be seen by faith. This was by no means just a Christian phenomenon. There was also a robust Jewish theological tradition—Aquinas often cited "Rabbi Moses" Maimonides—just as there were many Islamic commentators. The Islamic world in those days was a center of learning and culture with a thriving Aristotelian tradition of science, medicine, law, and philosophers like Avicenna and Averroes. Indeed the rebirth of learning in thirteenth-century Europe to which Thomas Aquinas belonged was made possible by the influx of Islamic learning into Europe through Spain. There were plenty of cultural and religious wars in the Middle Ages, like the Crusades, but they were wars between one faith and another rather than wars between faith and reason.

THREE

Of course, the moderns thought that the reason things went so smoothly in the "age of faith"—even to think this is so is to entertain a romanticized idea of the situation—is the power relation between theology (the church) and philosophy. Things went well, rather the way things go seemingly smoothly in a marriage as long as the wife obeys her husband. But underneath all this order is a deep disorder, the moderns think, and the time had come to assert the rights of reason, of free and independent inquiry independent of the power of the church (faith), and of traditional authorities like Aristotle. The time had come for the "Age of Reason," where that is a bit of a *double entendre*, meaning both the historical epoch of reason and reaching the age of reason, when you are old enough to drive, drink, and make your own mistakes. The time had come to get out our telescopes (of course, Galileo had first to invent the telescope) and to see more closely just what was going on for ourselves, and to do so freely, without the priests (who do not know which end of a telescope to look through) telling us in advance what we are going to see. I am referring of course to the birth of modern science, to the age of Copernicus, Kepler, and Galileo, to the "Copernican revolution," the first really big test case in adjusting the tensions between theology and the more independent sphere of reason. Unhappily, the church made all the wrong moves and set off a war between faith and science that is still being waged today, where the debate about teaching evolution in the public schools has been re-enkindled. When the church put Galileo on trial, it forgot everything that Thomas Aquinas had taught about the relationship between God as the author of nature and natural processes. The condemnation of Galileo planted first a suspicion and then a widespread conviction among scientists that persists to this day that religious people have checked their rational faculties at the door and that you get to choose between thinking and believing, but you cannot do both at the same time.

Notice now that we have introduced a new player on the scene of the ancient contest between philosophy and theology—the natural sciences, a phenomenon that will succeed in getting both their attentions. We can no longer assume the interchangeability of "philosophy" and "reason" because philosophy has had to move over and share the turf of reason with the newly emerging natural sciences. And while in the late seventeenth century Newton would still call his main work *Mathematical Principles of Natural Philosophy* (1687), the writing was on the wall. The gradual but irreversible process had begun of the particular sciences breaking off from philosophy that would eventually bring us to the point where we are today, where philosophy is the name of but one specialized, usually small department in modern academic institutions. There is even something slightly anachronistic about the word "philosophy" today. It is something we associate with ancient Greeks, and we find it a little surprising to learn that there still are such beings walking around these days, which is like finding out that a species that we thought extinct is only highly endangered.

What happened in modernity is that the relationship between faith and reason was reversed, and now the principle that whoever is in power abuses it was visited upon the church and, what is much worse, since the church often enough deserves the grief it gets, upon God. It is not so much that theology and religious faith were driven out of court as that they were hauled into court, made to stand before the tribunal of reason, made to answer for themselves in terms that do not suit or fit religious life or theological reflection, with the result that they were reduced to something less than themselves. Religion and theology were made to answer for themselves before the "Court of Final Appeals," where the sitting judge bore the name of "Principle of Sufficient Reason," which meant: anything that claims to be must possess sufficient reason for being.

Let us start with René Descartes, which is where most historians start when they want to find a clear marker for the beginnings of modernity. It is a good choice; Descartes was a very modern man indeed who was at one and the same time a philosopher, a mathematician, and a theoretical physicist, and who sought to put the disorderly house of philosophy in order by having it imitate the success of mathematics. Like good mathematicians, Descartes said, philosophers should start methodically with self-evident axioms and proceed from there with deductive rigor to firmly held conclusions. To this end Descartes set out in his famous *Meditations on First Philosophy* to put everything in doubt, not permanently and not out of some sense of perversity or despair, of course, but methodically, precisely in order to discover what was absolutely certain, that is, what could not possibly be put in doubt, and to build everything else on that firm foundation. This is the start of what the philosophers called "foundationalism."

Sociologically, what Descartes was doing as a philosopher corresponded to the tremors that were rattling European culture as a result of the Copernican revolution. At points of crisis and transition like this, everything seems uncertain, and Descartes wanted to resolve those tremors and put everything on a truly firm basis. This he did by way of the famous argument: Even if I doubt, I who doubt must think, and if I think, I must therefore exist *(cogito, ergo sum)*. And from that foundation he set about rebuilding the edifice of knowledge. At the same time, the Reformation theologians were abandoning the plains of philosophy as worldly folly—back to Saint Paul on the foolishness of philosophy (1 Cor. 1)—and retreating to the higher grounds of faith, the Scriptures, and the inner space of private conscience. The divorce had begun, and the two have been living in separate quarters ever since.

Although Descartes proved the existence of God three times in his *Meditations* and dedicated his book to his Jesuit teachers, and even though his famous *cogito* was reminiscent of something Saint Augustine had said: If I am deceived, I am *(si fallor, sum)*, the church felt obliged to condemn his writings. The church had yet to learn that the charm and the power of its old authoritarian way of doing things was fading fast and that it was going to have to learn to respect the new sense of freedom of individual conscience in modernity, to get out of the business of condemning everything new and different, and to respond more thoughtfully and with persuasive arguments to the evolving world around it. But you can see what made the church uneasy. Descartes was engaging in a kind of *pure philosophizing*, exercising a pure philosophical *autonomy*, speaking with an unprecedented *freedom*, and demanding that things present their credentials before being admitted across the borders of reality, the spirit of which frightened the church half to death. What Kant would later on call the "maturation" of the Western mind was at hand—and the parents were panicking.

While the Cartesian (as in Des "Cartes") experiment was a marvelous deployment of the philosophical imagination and an immensely important act of liberation of thought from the tutelage of ecclesiastical and theological authoritarianism, it has come under almost relentless fire in the last century of philosophy, and in my view rightly so. My specific concern here is to see what became of God in Descartes' thought. Jean-Luc Marion, arguably the greatest living Cartesian scholar, and also arguably the greatest living philosophical theologian—although you will get an argument about that, depending on your philosophy and your theology—singles out something that looks innocent enough on the surface but turns out to be a crucial symptom of a deep swerve in the way modernity was thinking about God. Descartes established what would become standard practice among the moderns, to refer to God as the "cause of itself" *(causa sui)* whereas for Aquinas, God is the "first cause uncaused," the cause of everything else but himself without a cause. If something else were the cause of God, then God's cause would be greater than God. Then why not say that God is the cause of himself? Because that makes no sense. It would mean that a thing gives itself what it does not have—like lifting yourself up by your own bootstraps, or bringing yourself into being where you previously did not exist. To be your own cause is to be before your time, to be there ahead of your own coming into being, which you then bring about; it is to be there already when you are not there yet. Like being your own father or mother. And that makes no sense. But while such things are impossible for us, surely they are possible with God, for whom all things are possible? Not so fast, answered Aquinas. It makes no sense to say that God can do things that make no sense, not when God is the very height of sense and meaning and truth. It pays God no real compliment. It makes much more sense to say that nothing is the cause of God, that God is the first cause of everything else but God himself is uncaused, that God exists in and of himself, as pure and sheer eternal necessity, without beginning and without end.

If that all seems very clear, why would Descartes, who as a Catholic was well-instructed in the ins and outs of medieval philosophy, say such a thing? The reason, Marion answers, is that Descartes wanted a world that was thoroughly rational, and for him that meant one that obeyed in every respect the axioms that reason lays down, in which the principles of reason held pride of place. The world is the sphere of things that meet the demands of reason, that pass muster under the inspection that reason makes, that are able to present their papers in order to be allowed to cross the border from fiction to reality. As a mathematician and a physicist, for example, Descartes said that, much as we love the odors and colors and feels of physical objects, as strictly rational beings we have to give them up and concede that the only thing that is "really out there," "objectively" (this was an entirely new way to talk) is mass and velocity, while such pleasant things as blue or sweet are strictly subjective or private sensations. Why so? Because the measure of physical reality is what is mathematically measurable, and the only thing you can measure about "blue" is light waves, or about "loud" is the frequency of sound waves. Reason does not take what is out there on face value and then adjust to it. On the contrary, by reason we mean the authority to determine what is out there in the first place and to set the standards to which things have to measure up. That is what the "Age of Reason," the "Enlightenment," means. It all has to do with who has the "authority" and the power— faith or reason.

So it would be no exaggeration to say that Descartes was very much attached to the principles of reason, which as necessary, universal, and ahistorical, held unconditionally and without exception. Notice what is grabbing all the headlines here: not God, but reason. While the medieval philosophers once described reason as a *capax dei*, a capacity for God, a finite capacity for the infinite, Kant would shortly define reason in the *Critique of Pure Reason* as a "faculty of principles." What is eternally necessary and unconditional is reason, and if God is going to get a share in all that glory, it will be because God measures up to the principles and standards reason sets. Of course, for Descartes and for most early modern thinkers, God does. God passes all these tests *summa*, nay *maxima cum laude*. God scores perfectly on all of reason's tests. The statement "God exists" is true because God meets the standards reason sets for a statement to be true. Descartes was a completely orthodox Catholic with no interest in over-throwing the substantive conclusions of classical theology. Instead, Descartes was interested in proofs and method and setting things out with the fixity and surety of mathematics itself; that is what is revolutionary about his thinking. God meets all the standards reason sets, *including the principle of causality*. God is the cause of himself, because everything has a cause—and reason cannot give in on that point, cannot give up one of its principles—including God, who is uniquely the cause of himself. The medievals said that a cause communi-cates something to the effect that the effect of itself does not have (like being or motion), so nothing can be the cause of itself. But Descartes reformulated the principle of causality to mean there must be as much reality in the cause as in the effect, and as there is as much reality in God (the effect), namely, an infinite amount, as there is in God (the cause), God is no exception to this principle. The cause must be suf-ficient to produce the effect, and the uniquely infinite God is the one and only sufficient cause of God. If you look closely at the main proof Descartes is using in the Third Meditation, you will see it is a modernist variation on Saint Anselm's ontolog-ical argument, even though the spirit of Anselm's discourse is entirely gone. Shortly after Descartes, Gottfried Wilhelm von Leibniz formulated the "principle of sufficient reason," which is that nothing is unless it has a sufficient reason for being. The court is in session. Reason functions like a judge, or like a border guard issuing passes into reality only to things that pass its tests, including, God help us, God.

Notice what has happened here. God, the subject matter of theology par excellence, has come under the principles of reason, which are the jurisdiction of philosophy, rather than reason coming under God, the subject matter of theology. God has to stand in line like everyone else; what's fair is fair. Both finite and infinite being must pass in review under reason's scrutiny. God, in effect, gets in line, gets shrunk down, is cut to fit the principles of reason, and theology now becomes a "particular discipline" (no longer the queen) monitored by the higher principles of philosophy, which keeps watch over all knowledge and all science generally. But from a theological point of view, no matter how high you heap your praise of God, if that praise is based upon measuring God by the tests written and administered by reason, you are debasing God, even if God comes out first in his class by your standards. In theology, where God is first, last, and always, God is the one who sets the standards, not the one who is measured by them, even if God is up to the test. What theologians ultimately worry about when it comes to the philosophers is that they have a tin ear for religion and theology, that they do not understand its distinctive discourse and form of life, so that even when they are offering arguments on behalf of God, the philosophers are still getting it wrong.

The medieval philosophers and theologians certainly sub- scribed to what they called the "first principles," principles that are evident "through themselves," but they neither for- mulated nor codified these principles so explicitly, nor did they cluster them into an autonomous body of absolute philo- sophical knowledge. From the medieval point of view, the moderns were getting it backwards. The reason the principles of reason have such splendid luminosity and are so convinc- ingly self-evident is that they are reflecting the splendid luminosity of God's own being. To say that God "obeys" these principles is to put it all perversely, wrongheadedly, even impiously, like saying that a father resembles his son instead of the other way around. For, on the contrary, as reflections of God's being, necessity, and truth, the principles obey God. As

Saint Augustine said, when we human beings think something true, that is in our own imperfect way to think something about God, who *is* truth. God is not "true" but Truth. God is the original; the principles are the reflections in the water.

All of this focusing—some might say fetishizing—of reason comes to a head in Kant who invented the idea of "critical philosophy," philosophy as "epistemology," as critique of knowledge, a kind of intellectual police sent into the world to supervise and regulate the several workings of reason. In Kant's critical philosophy, philosophy reaches a height of prestige to which it will never again pretend, as the science of science itself, the knowledge of knowledge itself, before which theology, hat in hand, will have to present itself for routine inspection. But Kant might also be viewed as philosophy's famous last stand. For Kant is already making a fateful concession, that all genuinely new knowledge comes through the sciences. By setting philosophy up a notch, as a higher science that oversees science, setting its conditions and limits, he means to give philosophy a supervisory position, but he also effectively removes philosophy from the action, like a restaurant critic who doesn't cook! Philosophy concerns a higher level epistemological theory of science, but it has abandoned the real world to the sciences. Where philosophy was once the word we used to describe our knowledge of the real world, now it is a word we use to describe knowledge itself, and we leave the world to the sciences. Kant has taken philosophy out of the game of knowing the world and made it into a kind of referee who judges whether the ball has remained in bounds. Philosophy has become a second order reflective science, while the sciences that deal with the world, that discover something about reality, are just called "science" pure and simple. Kant is the end of philosophy's great beginning in Socrates and typifies the point we have reached today where philosophy is a relatively minor and esoteric voice, a course you might take in college ("to round yourself out") if it fits your schedule as a business or computer science major.

In any event, Kant's critical philosophy consisted of three great "critiques" of "reason," which map out the territory of reason as the final and encompassing domain within which we rational beings live our lives. Our true essence is to be a "rational being," while being "human" is a merely zoological category describing an empirical species of speaking bipeds here on earth. Kant draws three great maps, the three critical domains, of what we can know, of what we ought to do, and of what we judge and esteem (like artistic and natural beauty). By a critique he meant something cartographical (Cartesian!), staking off the boundaries of the various domains of knowledge, ethics, and art, setting off their limits, and making sure everyone plays in bounds. The result of this kind of rigorous border drawing was to isolate pure and value-free knowledge, a pure ethical command or imperative that had no content beyond its purely rational-imperative form, and pure art, devoid of cognitive or ethical content. It was a short step from Kant to the next generation, so to speak, to defend knowledge for knowledge's sake, duty for duty's sake, art for art's sake, like three islands in an archipelago. The first critique tells us what is, the second what ought to be, the third how pleasant it would be if these two cohered with each other.

But so far nothing about God and religion. That is because for Kant, God and religion do not have their own island, their own domain or space or playing field; they must build their house of worship on someone else's property. God does not belong to the sphere of knowledge because the domain of knowledge is controlled by the physical sciences, and the idea of God as a supersensible cause simply does not register in natural science; it never gets a footing. The argument used by Anselm, and rehabilitated by Descartes, is an ineffectual wrestling with concepts, concepts that have lost their traction because they have been removed from the empirical world where they have their only legitimate application. So like Aquinas but unlike Descartes, Kant rejected

Anselm's argument. But even if he had accepted it, the theological life has gone out of Anselm's discourse and the point has been lost. Such a pure philosophical being that would have conformed to the Kantian standard of proof would have next to nothing to do with what Saint Anselm was proposing.

Then is God a simple phantasy for Kant? Indeed not. To put its best foot forward, the God of Kant, the God of the Enlightenment theology, or "natural theology," which is also the God of the American founders—"Nature's God," mentioned in the Declaration of Independence[4]—was meant to be a God as a kind of common and more or less self-evident datum of human intelligence, liberated from any particularism, any dogmatic or confessional theology (illustrated in Gotthold Lessing's famous drama *Nathan the Wise*). This is a God and a theology that anyone with a head on his shoulders could understand, which is basically the God revealed in the order of nature and the God who supports the moral order. Accordingly, Kant made two provisions for God. First of all, the idea of God plays a "regulative" role for Kant, and this belongs to the third critique, that of pleasant and reassuring judgment, because for all the world, the world looks as if it is governed by a wise order, which implies a wise governor. While that cannot be a piece of scientific knowledge, because it is a nonempirical hypothesis, it is a useful heuristic device, a fruitful "as if." By this Kant meant that it would stimulate research and advance the cause of science if every time science comes upon a phenomenon that needs explaining, it should ask itself, "Suppose this had been put there by a wise governor, what would the governor have had in mind and why would the governor have put it there?" Kant found a second role for God in the second critique, as not only nature's God but also the moral God, where the idea of God comes attached to the idea of duty. We are all visited by an unconditional command to do our duty. Whether we like it not, and whether it will make us happy or not, the "thou shalt" of moral duty rings unconditionally, uncompromisingly, non-negotiably, in our ears. A religious person is someone who understands that imperative as a command of God, a God who sees to it that in the end doing your duty and happiness, which in and of themselves run on separate tracks, end up at the same station. What then is religion? Religion is ethics; it is doing your duty where the voice of duty or conscience is taken as the voice of God.

So Kant's God, the Enlightenment's God, corresponded to the enduring intuitive link of God with the natural and moral order, and hence with a kind of natural or rational faith in that link, in "rational theology." What about the rest of religion—the sacraments, the dogmas, the liturgies, the hymns and candles, the miracles, and sacred stories? They are superstition. Religion as a whole must be supervised by reason. It must be kept within the limits of reason alone, which determines that the rational content of religion is ethics. That is the objective part of religion; the rest is a subjective buzz, like "blue" or "sweet," and while a lot of it is harmless, a lot of it is dangerous, because insofar as religion is not purely rational, people start getting crazy things inside their heads. They hear voices and start marching not to universal imperatives but to commands that no one but they can hear. They abandon the rational conduct of life, substitute magical incantations for dealing with reality, see spirits that no one else can see, and ultimately fall into divisive, destructive, and violent conflicts with other people with differing dogmatic beliefs and differing guiding spirits. But if they stick to their purely rational content, which is ethics, the various religions can achieve consensus. That is the point of Lessing's drama.

While this Enlightenment rational theology linked God up with certain basic human intuitions, the effect was to put God in such a vulnerable position that it was only a matter of time until someone would come along and lop God off, on the grounds that natural science and human ethics, that is, reason, could really get along fine, thank you very much, without this extra hypothesis, which tended more and more to look like an unnecessary supplement. That is pretty much what happened in the nineteenth century, which is the first time that atheism really got into gear. The nineteenth century produced a series of shocks with which religion and theology are still dealing. The shock delivered by evolutionary science, which reminded us of our biological roots, and the three-fold shock of the three great atheistic critiques of religion: as a false antidote to the misery of poverty (Karl Marx), as a psychological illusion (Sigmund Freud), as an expression of our resentment against the power of the strong (Friedrich Nietzsche).

By the end of the nineteenth century, theology and religious faith were on the run, at least among the intellectuals. God and religion were being thoroughly routed by the autonomy of reason. Philosophy itself was reacting, not acting, constantly ceding more ground to the natural sciences and looking around for something it could call its own. The church, it turns out, was not nervous about Descartes without reason.[5]

Faced with these developments, the theologians in the nineteenth century had little option but to retreat and retrench. Conceding the ground of knowledge to the natural sciences, they made a move not unlike the one that Pascal made against Descartes ("the heart has reasons that reason does not know"[6]): they relocated religion in new quarters in the sphere of "feeling." They took heart in Romanticism, a counter-movement to the Enlightenment, which stressed the creative power of the imagination over and against the confining power of reason with all of its borders and rules. The greatest theological figure of the time was Friedrich Schleiermacher, the father of liberal theology, who traced religion back to a "feeling of absolute dependence," where feeling was given new credentials and special access to God, functioning like a ticket or pass to the eternal and the infinite— thereby overcoming the arid rationalism and deism by which theology was threatened in the Enlightenment. It was in the world of Romantics that these anti-moderns also took a new look at the "Christian (read Catholic) Middle Ages," which suddenly seemed to them like an enchanted forest—the age of chivalry, full of knights and faith and fair princesses—before it had been disenchanted by the Enlightenment.

At the end of the nineteenth century, religion was on the run and seemed to belong to times gone by. The exploding new technology, the rise of capitalism, the newly emerging mass means of communication and transportation, and the forces of scientific naturalism were in the ascendency. It was the philosopher Nietzsche who summed it all up: God is dead. Thus spoke the nineteenth century.

FOUR

---

ut a funny thing happened on the way to the funeral.
The wheels came off the Enlightenment. In a way that
none of the positivists and naturalists of the nineteenth
century would ever have guessed, it turned out that the
Enlightenment had done all the good it was going to do and
that it was necessary to frame things out differently. That is
the development to which I want to turn to now. But before I
do, let me first go on record. My own view is that
Enlightenment or modernity is a necessary phase, an essential
course correction, in working out a satisfactory reconciliation
of the competing claims of faith and reason. Religious people
hold their faith to be the most precious thing they have, and
well they should, but everything depends upon understanding
the faith that is in you, on thinking it through and thinking it
out, in dialogue with others and with everything else that God
has given us. That is why theology proceeds without
philosophy at great personal risk to itself.

The great strength of the Enlightenment view of religion
and revelation lay in two points of emphasis: (1) In the conduct of human affairs we should keep our eye on what we all
have in common and not emphasize divisive "revelations"
granted to some and withheld from others. The Christian

Right keeps praying that we go back to the religious vision of the American founders, but they should be careful what they are praying for, lest their prayers be answered. The American founders were men of the Enlightenment, and they would have been appalled by the strident sectarian agenda of the Christian Right and by its way of riding roughshod over the differences of opinion that the founders set out to protect from oppression. (2) God has not given the faithful revelation and only revelation. God has planted a head on our shoulders and put eyes in that head, and so the full job description of a believer is to be a thinking believer or a believing thinker (the emphasis depends on whom you are talking to or sometimes just what day it is). God has given us a revelation in the very widest sense, not just the book of Revelation, but the visible things of this world that tell us of the invisible things of God (Rom. 1:20). That is why philosophy and theology have to learn to get along. We make no progress with God by beating up on the world God made—which Elohim declared to be good five times and then summed it up a sixth time by saying *very* good—or the faculties God has given us in order to know the world. The full revelation, revelation in the most ample and generous sense, includes everything that comes to us by faith *and* reason, through theology *and* philosophy, sacred science *and* secular science. In the widest and most generous sense of (uncapitalized) "enlightenment," there are many lights, and the light of reason and the light of faith are among our leading lights. God bless both of them together. God bless the "and" and keep it safe.

So while I am about to shift into a critical attitude toward modernity, I do not want to set myself in simple opposition to modernity, which is, I think, what happened in Romanticism. I am no more opposed to modernity than I am to air-conditioning or high-definition television. I am no more opposed to modernity than I am to freedom of speech and freedom from religious authoritarianism. I am no more opposed to modernity than I am to the rights of each person, however humble, white or black, male or female, Western or non-Western, to a full and free and happy life, which is the political ideal that eventually surfaces under the power of the ideals of the Enlightenment. Furthermore, as far as I am concerned, I am happy to let reason knock itself out trying to think things through as best it can on its own terms. Modernity is as important to us as maturity. It is a stage in our maturation and Kant was right about that, and we will rue the day we ever took a simple stand against it.

But there is such a thing as *hubris*, overreaching pride, failing to know ourselves well enough to know our own limits, just as most teenagers think they know everything until they become parents themselves and acquire a new respect for what their parents really know after all and how much they still need their help and experience. So as impressed as I am with the spirit of modern critique and suspicion, I also insist that we should not hesitate to be critical of this critique, to suspect this suspicion, and to advocate a more reasonable and uncapital-ized idea of reason. Let me be clear: I am interested not in the abolition of modernity but in the continuation of modernity *by another means*, and that is how I interpret what is nowadays called postmodernity, which I will discuss shortly, since for better or worse, postmodernity is the condition under which we today conduct the business of philosophy and theology, of science and art, of politics and religion, of just about everything.

In the twentieth century, the enthusiasm for "pure reason" and a pure Enlightenment was tempered, and what the Enlightenment called "reason" came under fire from many sides. Just what went wrong in the Enlightenment can be seen by looking at its politics. Politically, as I just said, the ultimate political ideal emerging from the Enlightenment is a radical egalitarianism, a respect for the human individual, and a respect for people with differing views. However, the

Enlightenment and its ideas about reason were often its own worst enemy in terms of realizing that ideal. As often as not, what the Enlightenment delivered was imperialism, not egalitarianism. Because the Enlightenment had too narrow an idea of what "reason" means and too chauvinistic an idea of where it is to be found, for the longest time it placed the crown of reason on white male European heads, whose duty it was, it said with its eyes cast heavenward, to spread Euro-white maledom around the globe. The most famous case in point is the "discovery" of the "new world" (I place these words in scare quotes to acknowledge the people who already lived there), and the subsequent genocide practiced upon the native peoples of the Americas, north and south, in the name of European civilization. To this day, the indigenous peoples of the Western world, as well as women of all races, and non-Westerners of every stripe, endure and have endured enormous suffering to drive home the full length and breadth of the egalitarian forces that the Enlightenment set loose. Politically, the latent energies that had first grouped themselves under the flag of "Enlightenment" clearly needed a new configuration (and a lot less flag waving).

But apart from the politics, as a pure philosophical idea, its core idea of "reason" would prove to be overreaching, an exaggeration, a mistake, and it would be attacked on many fronts in the twentieth century. But the attack had already begun in the nineteenth century itself, not only in the Romantics' outright rejection of Enlightenment, but in G. W. Hegel himself, a towering German philosopher who is a companion of Kant in German philosophy the way Aristotle is a companion of Plato in Greek philosophy. Hegel was the first great philosopher of history, the philosopher who put history on philosophy's map. Hegel insisted against the Enlightenment that the ideas and ideals of "pure reason" have a coefficient in time and history where they are embodied in the flesh and blood, the sweat and tears, of concrete peoples.

So Hegel introduced a distinction between what he called *Verstand*, abstract understanding, and *Vernunft*, the more concrete embrace of a robustly *historical* reason. Abstract understanding is one-sided, purely formal and ahistorical, and how right he was. Descartes labored under a narrowly ahistorical and purely mathematical idea of reason; Kant shrunk reason down to formal consistency and universality; and the British John Locke and David Hume confined reason to its blunter empirical applications. Against all this, Hegel showed that reason unfolds and develops in time, passing through several forms *(Gestaltungen)*, and that it is realized in different ways, in different times and places. The pure abstract "morality" of Kant, the formal universality of doing yourself only what can be universalized into a rule for everyone, Hegel said, must melt into the concrete universality of what he called ethical life *(Sittlichkeit)*, that is, the real rules and rich customs and concrete practices of cultural and social life in which rational morals are actually embodied.

Hegel represented an important and irreversible advance on Enlightenment. But one Enlightenment ideal that Hegel had no intention of giving up was the idea that reason forms a "system," a comprehensive whole, that it seeks an ultimate goal or end *(telos)* that governs all the particular elements in the system. From the point of view of what is now called the postmodern, that affection for system was a fatal flaw. For Hegel, what unfolds in time and history is a deep rationality or rational principle, what he called the "absolute," which works its way out beneath and seeks its goals through the twists and turns that history seems to take on the surface. God writes straight with crooked lines. That kind of thinking became part of the problem, not part of the solution, for it only served to perpetuate pretty much the same "totalizing," all-encompassing grip of "reason," now in the form of a historical reason that the Enlightenment had first proposed. So, for example, the Hegelian is committed by this view to say that the Holocaust is all part of a plan administered by the hidden hand of history's *Vernunft*. In this we see Hegel represents only partial progress in twisting free from Enlightenment.

What went wrong in Hegel can be seen in what Hegel has to say about religion and theology, not only because those are our special concerns in these pages but because the religious reaction against Hegel has a lot to do with the emergence of the postmodern. Hegel said that Christianity is the absolute religion and the absolute truth, which sounds like a splendid start as far as the theologians are concerned. That was the good news. The bad news is what Hegel meant. Theologians are rightly wary of philosophers bearing gifts! He was saying that Christianity is the absolute truth in a pictorial form, that it says something very true but that the particular terms in which it is does so are not quite true, are not the whole truth, are not as true as true can be. The word he used to describe religion's truth is *Vorstellung*, which means a representation or depiction or even a picture; it is related to the word *Darstellung*, which means an "exhibition" or presentation, say, of paintings. So Hegel was saying that Christianity is a pretty picture, the truth in a "pictorial" mode. As opposed to what? To the unvarnished truth of a philosophical concept that clears up what the storyteller was trying to say.

Take the story of Christmas that we find in Matthew and Luke, of Jesus born of a virgin, laid in a manger because there is no room in the inn, of the songs of angels summoning shepherds to the scene, of wise men coming from the East, etc. That makes for a powerful and moving story and the most beautiful greeting cards—Christmas is the answer to the prayers of Hallmark cards. This story is to be taken seriously but not literally. For what it says in the mode of narratival imagination is that God has become immanent in the world and that the world is the unfolding of God's life in space and time. In the first phase of religion, which Hegel called the religion of the Father, God is taken to be transcendent and wholly other, a distant power, a pure command, not unlike an absolute Eastern monarch; Judaism is his example. In the second phase, the religion of the Son, God becomes man by becoming a particular man, Jesus, whose empirical particularity has to break up (the Crucifixion), like a seed that must break up in order to germinate. Only then can we enter the final phase, the religion of the Spirit, in which God's life among us may spread to all, and we all come to understand that history is the unfolding of God's life in time. In other words, Christian theology is simply a metaphorical way of speaking about a metaphysical situation, which goes like this. The natural world is the expression of the divine life in an objective manner, in the material objects that make up the natural world, and human culture is the expression of the divine life in cultural and historical life—God's autobiography in time, as Hegel once put it. Philosophy is the highest form of cultural or spiritual life in which the absolute comes back to itself in self-knowledge. What Hegel was saying drew strength from the results of the newly emergent "historical criticism" in nineteenth-century biblical studies, that is, the attempt to discover the "historical Jesus," to sort out exactly what was historically verifiable about the New Testament and what had been added on by the speculations of the "theologians," not only the latter day theologians like Augustine but the proto-theologians already at work in the New Testament itself. This came to a famous head in Rudolph Bultmann's call to "de-mythologize" the New Testament: "The whole conception of the world which is presupposed in the preaching of Jesus as of the New Testament generally is mythological; i.e., the conception of the world as being structured in three stories, heaven, earth and hell; the conception of the intervention of supernatural powers in the course of events; and the conception of miracles . . ."[7] This was basically what Hegel had set about doing. To this day, "theologians" and biblical "historians" do not get along with each other very well. The historians think the theologians twist the words of the Scriptures to their own dogmatic ends, and the theologians think the historians do not believe a thing.

Hegel is also the progenitor of a philosophical theology that later on came to be known as "panentheism," an American theological movement also called "process theology" spurred by the British philosopher Alfred North Whitehead. Panentheism is not a simple pantheism which treats everything as flat-out divine, but is the notion that all things are *in* God and God is in all things, that each and everything in some way expresses or instantiates the divine principle and that God on his part has no separate existence or transcendent reality apart from the world.

Every time Søren Kierkegaard heard things like this from the Hegelians, he howled in pain and the cry he sent up, the impressive body of literature that issued from his injured heart, is one of the great contributions to Western religious literature, to Western literature period. To the notion that Christianity is something to be gotten by Hegelian metaphysics, that faith is a twilight state to be surpassed beyond by gaining entry to the clarity of conceptual thinking provided by German metaphysics, Kierkegaard responded with the best means he had at his disposal—with satire and laughter. If philosophy is the highest form of cultural or spiritual life, and German philosophy is the highest form of philosophy, and Hegel is the highest philosopher, that must mean, Kierkegaard mused, that when God descends into the world of nature and clears his head in cultural-spiritual life, he wakes up as a German philosopher (guess who!).

For all his satire, Kierkegaard made a philosophically incisive critique that reshaped the history of European philosophy after him. Kierkegaard is an illustrative case of a religious attack, or counter-attack, upon philosophy that produces not the end of philosophy, but a new philosophy-under-attack. Kierkegaard said in brief that Christianity is the Cross, is

Christ and Christ crucified, and there was not a Hegelian philosopher in all of his native Denmark, and he would have wagered in all of Europe, who as far as he could tell was anywhere near to catching up to faith, let alone surpassing it. It took Abraham a whole lifetime to learn the ways of faith, and Abraham was the father of faith, and one could spend one's whole lifetime trying to become a Christian and never get that far. But how awesome are the Hegelian philosophers. All hail to the Hegelians who have not only gotten as far as Abraham and Christianity but also have managed to surpass them, and this at a relatively early age and with all the comforts of a well-paid position at the university. Kierkegaard was the main nineteenth-century background figure for Karl Barth, one of the towering geniuses of Christian theology in the twentieth century, the father of "neo-orthodoxy," who also insisted mightily on the scandal and the contradiction that the New Testament gives to the "world." Along with Nietzsche—who also made a jest of German metaphysics, those pale morticians, those conceptual embalmers, those chalk-dusty dabblers in the last cloudy evaporating streaks of reality, as he called them—Kierkegaard set the stage for the twentieth-century critique of "totalization," of totalizing reason, be it pure or historical, that eventually gave the word "postmodern" its currency.

F I V E

There are both theological (Kierkegaard) and anti-theological (Nietzsche) motives behind the emergence of the postmodern. But no matter how you cut it, if the main drift of modernity was toward secularization, it is inevitable that something that gets to be called *postmodern* will provide an opening for the *postsecular*, a word that has recently gained some currency in tandem with postmodern. If the long arms of the modern and the secular are overreaching, what then are the possibilities for theology in the postmodern situation? What is postmodern theology? What is theology in the postmodern situation? Does not theology today operate in a milieu that is, for better or for worse, postmodern, just as theology in the thirteenth century was deployed in the midst of an Aristotelian revival that swept over western Europe, and just as Augustine's theology was embedded in the world of late antiquity in which he lived? Theology has never existed in a vacuum, nor has philosophy, which is the strong suit of those theologians who insist on the "correlation" of theology and the surrounding culture. Theologies come to birth in a concrete time and culture and language, and, for better or worse, they come under the influence of the philosophy and culture of the day. Theologians give words to revelation by means of the words theologians are given to speak, and these words are given by the world in which they live.

For simplicity's sake, and I concede that I am simplifying to an extreme, I will single out three background ideas that shaped the postmodern situation. In *Being and Time* (1927), Martin Heidegger argued—here is where the impulse of Kierkegaard is palpable—that, as he put it, as soon as we come to be we find that we are already there. That seeming tautology actually says quite a lot. It means we can never get behind ourselves and see ourselves come into being, or that we can never get out of our skin and look down upon ourselves from above. We "always already" are the beings that we are, and rather than trying the impossible, to make a presuppositionless start à la Descartes, we should realize that we are in truth shaped by the presuppositions we inherit. These presuppositions do not bind or blind us but rather give us our perspective, our angle of entry, enabling us to understand in the first place, giving shape to the way the world presents itself to us here and now. Angles do not bend and distort; they give us access. Without them, we would be lost, like those students who come to see their professors to discuss a topic for their research papers, with that deer-caught-in-the-headlights look on their faces, for while they have read the material (I am being generous), they lack the one thing necessary: an angle. Let us call that *the hermeneutical turn*.

Secondly, consider the simple fact that when Descartes wrote the *Meditations*, he was already *writing*. Once again, a tautology that packs a punch. That is, one of the presuppositions that escaped Descartes' notice when he set out to put everything in doubt, when he tried to clear the slate of his consciousness and start out from scratch, was that the entire work of doubt relied upon language. By using a word that he had borrowed from his Jesuit teachers, "meditations," he was trying to suggest a kind of inner soliloquy of the soul with itself, a solitary, world-less, naked and—here's the punchline—pre-linguistic contact of the soul with itself. But of course, everything he said, and I mean everything he *said*, every last *word* of it, was deeply embedded in the words he used that he had inherited from the Jesuits, and from the scholastic philosophers before them, and from his mother and father, and from the books he had read in school, and so on. So when Heidegger took to criticizing Descartes in *Being and Time*, Heidegger found it necessary to stand on his head in order not to talk like Descartes (or like anybody else for that matter), because Cartesian words like "consciousness," "objectivity," "doubt," "I," etc. are all loaded. They come equipped with ingrained grooves that will carry you down preestablished routes like a canoe in a rushing stream if you use them. Vocabularies are like keys that only fit in certain locks, tools that only do certain jobs, and they have a drift about them. They are public or cultural entities, and they are as deeply steeped in public presuppositions and prejudices and pre-established tendencies as modern produce is in herbicides and pesticides. As Ludwig Wittgenstein (a philosopher as important in Anglo-America as Heidegger is on the Continent) said, there is no such thing as a private language. Wherever Descartes starts his *Meditations*, it will be in the middle of a public language. There is no such thing as a pure, private, pre-linguistic sphere—and, once again, it is a misunderstanding of language even to seek one. We get somewhere in this business of thinking not by trying to shed language for some mythical, naked contact with the pre-linguistic, but by means of coming up with new, more complex and nuanced vocabularies, rather the way young parents brag about how complex their toddler's vocabulary has become as convincing evidence that their child is a genius. Or to come back to my previous analogy: what those students in search of help on research papers lack is "something to say." Let us call that the *linguistic turn.*

The final turn was taken when historian of science
Thomas Kuhn published *The Structure of Scientific Revolutions*
in 1962, which pointed out something fascinating but discon-
certing. Contrary to the myths of scientific positivism,
scientists are not pure bloodless observers recording information like automated information gathering systems; they are
flesh and blood people with hunches, intuitions, and strong
feelings. They do not passively record but actively project.
Furthermore, when something really new happens in science,
it is not because we add a new item of information to an old
list, but because the whole ensemble gets reconfigured. He was
led to say this from his study of the history of the Copernican
Revolution, which is the perfect example of what he meant.
The Copernican Revolution does not add new information
but rather reconfigures the same information as is available
under the Ptolemaic account, but makes it simpler, more elegant, more felicitously organized. You could assume that the
earth is at rest and all those heavenly bodies are moving
around us, but the mathematics would get knee-bendingly
complicated. Copernicus himself was a monk and—under
some pressures from the church—did not believe his own
theory himself. He just proposed it as a shorthand method of
predicting the movement of the stars for mariners, rather like
a mathematics teacher who shows the students a short cut
proof that will get the same results as the long proof. Kuhn
proposed that scientists work under overarching frameworks
he called "paradigms" that organize the particular experiments
that they make. Once in a very great while they run across an
anomaly so intractable that they cannot interpret it under the
old paradigm and find it simpler to completely rethink the paradigm of which they have been making use and switch to
another paradigm. And just like other innovations, the new
paradigm is attacked before it is embraced; the young graduate
students and assistant professors love it and the senior tenured
types hate it, and it does not take over until the latter retire,

die, or are eventually argued down loudly enough to get on the bandwagon. But at the start of the revolution, all the "evidence" is on the side of the old guard, and the avant-garde is proceeding mostly on insight or intuition. So things happen in Kuhn's "scientific revolution" in ways that much more closely resemble artistic or political revolutions than the advocates of scientific objectivity like to think. Let us call that a *revolutionary turn*.

With Kuhn, the tables start to turn—now it's not religion that is accused of mythologizing, but the apostles of scientific objectivity. The nineteenth-century positivists would have fainted dead away if they ever heard this. Kuhn was not, of course, coming out against scientific objectivity; he was just redescribing it. He said "objectivity" is not some sort of eternal knowledge; it is just the kind of thing you get in "normal" science, that is, in science that is being practiced under a settled paradigm, as most science is. But in times of scientific crisis, which are and should be rare, things are much more up for grabs than the Enlightenment ever dared allow itself to think. Nor was Kuhn coming out against "reason"; he was just redescribing reason in terms of the much more reasonable idea of having "good reasons" for thinking one thing rather than another, but to do so without pretending to have a piece of eternity in your pocket or an algorithm up your sleeve to settle all debates conclusively.

All of that effectively put a lot of what the Enlightenment was trying to sell us on the run, and good riddance. Good riddance to the idea of pure worldless and solipsistic subjects, to the ideal of pure presuppositionless science, to a pure prelinguistic world, to pure objects, to pure consciousness, and to pure reason. Give us some good old-fashioned impure thoughts! The world is a lot more complicated than the moderns think, a lot messier, less well-programmed, less rule-governed, more open-ended and open-textured. It is a lot more like what James Joyce called a "chaosmos,"[8] by which he did not mean a simple disorder, a simple street-corner anarchy, but a chaos/cosmos, an order (cosmos) that is kept loose by a certain amount of disorder, which is the leaven in the order that allows it to reconfigure and reorganize, to move ahead, to shift, to engender new paradigms, languages, angles. The hermeneutical turn, the linguistic turn, and the revolutionary turn taken in a Kuhnian analysis of a science—that is to say, the collective idea that human thinking turns on the ability to move among shifting perspectives, vocabularies, and para-digms, none of which has dropped from the sky—make up what we will call the *postmodern turn*. The windows were beginning to open up in the world, allowing in various lights other than that of "pure reason," the light of faith, the life of grace, the play of art, the possibility of the things the Enlightenment thought impossible. New possibilities for religion and theology were about to emerge.

The moment was ripe for Jean-François Lyotard to put the word *postmodern* on the map, when in 1977 he defined it in *The Postmodern Condition* as "incredulity to meta-narratives." I say put it on the map because the term already enjoyed currency in architectural theory where it referred to an archi-tectural eclecticism that softened the harsh lines of modernist architecture by way of historical citations, like a modern building made of glass and steel but made to evoke the lines of a Gothic cathedral. The French phrase Lyotard used that got translated as "meta-narratives" was *grands récits*, "big stories," that is, large overarching accounts, "totalizing stories" (he was thinking of Hegel) that claimed things like "history is nothing but the unfolding of the absolute spirit," or "nothing but the unfolding of the laws of dialectical materialism," or nothing but the displaced desire for your mommy, or nothing but the resentment of the weak against the strong, or nothing but this, that, or the other thing. Enough of these "nothing buts." When Lyotard said "incredulity," it was a brilliant choice of words on his part. He did not say "refutation," which would require a big story of its own, one big enough to refute them. He was saying that these things are pretentious, that they have not proven themselves, and we just don't believe them anymore. They have become incredible and we have grown incredulous. Almost any careful look at the way things are done in science or the way they unfold in history reveals the shortcomings of such simplistic and overreaching stories. Postmodernism thus is not relativism or scepticism, as its uncomprehending critics almost daily charge, but minutely close attention to detail, a sense for the complexity and multiplicity of things, for close readings, for detailed histories, for sensitivity to differences. The postmodernists think the devil is in the details, but they also have reason to hope that none of this will antagonize God. For are not the modernists rather like the Shemites, furiously at work on the tower of Babel, on the "system," as Kierkegaard would say with biting irony, and are not the postmodernists following the lead of God, who in deconstructing the tower clearly favors a multiplicity of languages, frameworks, paradigms, perspective, angles? From a religious point of view, does not postmodernism argue that God's point of view is reserved for God, while the human standpoint is immersed in the multiplicity of angles?

S I X

Enter religion and theology, which should feel emboldened to show their hoary head in this new postmodern scene. You see now where I have been heading. Picking up on the idea of a "language game," a notion that was first proposed by Wittgenstein, Lyotard proposed an irreducible plurality of language games, each with its own rules, each with its own rights, so that there is no one "meta-language" (this was the expression that inspired the translation) into which the other first-order or object-languages could be translated. By a game he did not mean a form of amusement but perfectly serious business, namely a rule-governed activity that you could only learn by practicing and by agreeing to follow the rules. By insisting on the multiplicity of language games, Wittgenstein was resisting the idea that all these games can be translated into the currency of a normative meta-language. The multiple games allow things to be said that you can only get by learning the language, learning how things get done in that language, by "going native," as the anthropologists say. Moving between and among the several games is made possible by a kind of leap or switch, a paradigm switch, from one game to the next.

By the several languages, Wittgenstein did not mean French, German, and Spanish (the "natural languages") but the language games of science, art, ethics, politics, religion, etc. The integrity and idiosyncrasy of each language game must be respected. It would go against the idea of language games, and therefore against the very idea of language itself, to declare that everything that is going on in all the other languages can be translated into the language of just one of them, say, natural science. So if someone said that human compassion (ethics) is *nothing other than* a certain evolutionary coping mechanism (biology), that would be unfair play, a scientific reductionism, a reduction of the irreducible. That choice of the example from ethics, of course, is not a random selection, but a singling out of something typical of the main threat posed by modernity, the reduction of human values to scientific objects. Of course, the hegemony of science today corresponds to the hegemony formerly exercised by theology, which posed the major threat in pre-modernity. (Whoever has the power abuses the power.)

It does not pay to exaggerate. A lot of the postmodern philosophers are thorough-going secularists and their nineteenth-century hero and predecessor is not Kierkegaard but Nietzsche. Their interest in defusing the intimidating prestige of the natural sciences and in gaining a hearing for other forms of discourse is aimed at promoting their interest in art and literature, not religion. But the clear and unmistakable result of what even these very secular thinkers did, the unavoidable implication of what in my view they very successfully accomplished, was to gain a hearing for—God help us—religion and theology, a point that discomforts secularizing postmodernists every bit as much as it discomforts modernist critics of religion. When philosophers really have an axe to grind about theology, that axe trumps the distinction between modern and postmodern. When it comes to theology, some philosophers take no prisoners.

But the undeniable result of the postmodern turn was to make it possible for religious and theological discourse to assert its rights. Just like the language of art and ethics, religious discourse, too, constitutes its own irreducible "form of life," as Wittgenstein would have called it. That means that certain irreducible things get done there, certain things that could only get done by switching into the "language game" of religion, which includes uniquely discursive forms all its own—like prayer, which means not only talking *about* God but also talking *to* God. Addressing "God" can no longer be dismissed on the grounds that it represents a nonempirical hypothesis (naturalism, positivism), and it can no longer be reduced to ethics (Kant). The meaning of the name of God is ultimately lodged in the concrete life of religious communities where the name is deployed, in the form of life of people who use this name. The meaning of "theology" is to give words to this form of life, to unfold or explicate or interpret what is happening there and to try to line it up with what happens in the other forms of life. Religion constitutes an irreducible paradigm of its own, a language of its own, a perspective of its own.

And if religious discourse, then also theology. Notice that theology should always follow upon religion. A very good example of this is Augustine, who was both a bishop and a theologian. That is, he was a pastor and a homilist, a person intimately involved in the lives of the faithful and whose theology grew up in a living conversation with his congregation, which ensured that his theology was a conceptualization of a living faith. Nowadays, that paradigm has degenerated on both fronts. On the one hand, the bishops have become bureaucrats, financial officers, CEOs, fund-raisers, administrators, damage-control specialists, almost anything but theologians. The theologians, on the other hand, are busy getting tenure and promotion in academic institutions, writing papers that practically nobody can read except other academics, and they have next to no contact with the actual practice of faith in the churches. So there is an important divide between religion and academic theology that is not healthy for either party and that we should not overlook.

It now becomes apparent that in the postmodern turn the line between faith and reason needs to be differently drawn. In the age of faith, in a pre-modern view of things, faith had the authority and understanding works in its service. In the modern view, the tables were turned, and reason became the public and authoritative guide to human affairs, while faith was confined to a sphere of private freedom, where it would be safe (and kept out of the way). In either case, the relation was hierarchical, and the common assumption was that faith and reason are definably different from each other. But if we reflect upon the course of things taken in the postmodern turn, it is clear that this distinction between faith and reason has become more porous. Consider the case of a Kuhnian paradigm. In times of normal science, the young apprentices in science are initiated into a world structured by a common assumption or presupposition or, shall we say, a common scientific faith in the ruling paradigm. It has proven itself trustworthy in the past, and the experts are *confident*—that means they have *fides*, faith—in its fruitfulness in the future. The experience and the authority of the experts in turn inspire the confidence of the apprentice. By the same token, in moments of revolutionary science, we have a to-do with a crisis of faith. The old guard is sure, its faith is firm that the traditional paradigm can survive the palace coup, that classical assumptions still hold. But the avant-garde is equally sure that it is right, that while all the accumulated evidence in the journals and the textbooks support the traditional presuppositions, it is equally confident that the future is on its side. Allowing for the fact that we are talking about making different scientific arguments and seeking different experimental confirmations of their claims, what we have here is a battle between conflicting faiths.

The reason this notion of conflicting faiths is not simply a metaphor or a kind of casual analogy has to do with the hermeneutic turn. To understand is not a kind of pure staring at a pure object. True, we are constantly receiving input from the world, but whatever we receive is received in a manner that is suitable for the receiver who must make ready for the reception. Even the most elemental perception is structured around a moment of expectation that is then confirmed—or not. When we open the door, we expect to find a house within, not a wind-swept prairie; when we lift the telephone book, we expect to feel its weight; when we sink into a chair, we expect it to hold us up. The perceptual world is to an important extent a coherent set of expectations, what Heidegger called an ensemble of "interpretive fore-structures," by means of which we make our way around the world via felicitous assumptions, ways of "taking" things "as" such-and-such, where if we move it, lift it, use it, eat or drink it, or greet it with a friendly hello, our expectations are confirmed—or not. The reason for our confusion when we find ourselves in the midst of unfamiliar objects, if we visit a foreign culture, for example, is that we do not know what to expect next. We move about the conceptual world in much the same way as we move about the perceptual world, in virtue of certain pre-understandings, embedded conceptual frameworks, webs of concepts that map the world out in ways that the progress of research confirms—or fails to. We lend our trust in these interpretive fore-structures; we believe them, unless or until they are discredited. We trust them, we must because otherwise we would have to reinvent the wheel several times a day. The smooth flow of perceptual life—as well as the conceptual work of scientists in their labs or of historians rooting through dusty archives—depends upon having structures of anticipation in place that we trust and are eventually forced to revise, reform, or otherwise recast.

In other words, in the classical distinction between reason and faith, which has always lain at the root of the negotiations between philosophy and theology, each bargaining from what it took to be its position of strength, the assumption is that reason is a kind of seeing, seeing clearly, and faith is a kind of not seeing, of seeing in part and through a glass darkly, as Saint Paul said. No matter where you stand in the classical debate, whether you placed faith before reason with the pre-moderns, or subjected faith to reason with the moderns, you tended to think that seeing is one thing and believing (faith) is another. But the upshot of the shift effected by the hermeneutical-linguistic-paradigmatic turn is to introduce the idea of *seeing as*, which functions like something of a third term that tends to break the log jam in these negotiations and to make the distinction between the two even more porous. "Seeing as" weakens the idea of "pure seeing" defended in the camp of reason and strengthens the idea of "seeing in part" defended in the camp of faith. "Seeing as" gives faith a larger role to play in what was hitherto called reason and sends the negotiators on both sides in this classic debate back to the drawing board. So now I fear I must switch my allegiances. Where I thought the key lay in this little word "and" in our title, I have now been led to see or to believe, I am not sure which, that the laurels should go to this still smaller word "as," whose stature was magnified by Heidegger when he called it "the hermeneutical as."

I say this for two reasons. (1) However we end up describing *reason* (and therefore science and philosophy), we will have to concede that it is not seeing all the way down, that it involves an ongoing faith and trust in its ensemble of assumptions and presuppositions, which function like a set of anticipatory fore-structures that enable us to make our way around—a lab or an archive, a poem or an ancient language, an economic system or a foreign culture. To be rational is to project things in a tested and confirmed way, to cast them in a certain way, to have a "read" on things. The light of reason means to cast things in a certain light, to take things "as" such and such, one that opens up a certain space for exploration—

and one that we are ready to recall as soon as it outlives its use-fulness and our faith in it is shaken. So *seeing is starting to look something like believing*. (2) By the same token, to have *faith* in something is not darkness and not-seeing all the way down. On the contrary, one will not be able to see at all without a certain faith, if we do not have a take, an "as," an angle, a per-spective, a vocabulary that we believe and trust. To believe is to take something "as," and to proceed with some confidence in our perspective, in order that we may see and understand. So *believing is starting to look a lot like seeing*. The idea is not to have a faith-free seeing, or a presuppositionless understanding, but to find the right presuppositions, the right assumptions, the right take, the right vocabulary that will throw the right light on things and enable us to see what is going on. The idea is to discern what to believe if we are to see.

If that is so, if I am right about that, then that allows me to formulate my third thesis, which is perhaps the strongest of all. The distinction between philosophy and theology is not what we thought it was all along; it is not what has been clas-sically described as the distinction between faith and reason, where reason sees and faith does not quite see. Rather, *the distinction between philosophy and theology is drawn between two kinds of faith*, by which I mean two kinds of "seeing as." It is rooted in the distinction between a common or philosophical faith, the complex web of presuppositional structures that is built right into every human enterprise, into what we call knowledge and what we call action, and another or second kind of faith, a more particular or determinate kind of faith, a specifically religious faith, where by "religious" I mean the sort of "confessional" faith that marks off Catholics from Protestants. The distinction between philosophy and theology is between two kinds of interpretative slants, two kinds of interpretations that are inwardly structured by the sort of faith at work in each. Faith, on this account, turns out to have a stronger hand to play, which is why I said a while back that the pre-moderns were onto something important. For faith is an elemental form of human life, a basic ingredient in our existence, as necessary as the air we breathe, and it proves to be an indispensable requirement for philosophy as well as for theology, which it turns out differ from each other in virtue of the difference between the faith that is in them, that is in each of them.

SEVEN

I would now like to illustrate this point, my third thesis about the wider sweep of faith in postmodernity, by examining a kind of test case that I will call, with planned impudence, the atheistic Augustinianism of Jacques Derrida. Notice that I am trying out this bold hypothesis with Augustine, not Thomas Aquinas. Augustine represents a more interesting possibility for postmodern theology, and the reason for this is that he had a more porous idea of the relationship between faith and reason. Augustine was convinced that his faith was the only way he could come to understand what was going on in his life. Aquinas thought while faith and reason fit together like hand and glove, still hands are hands and gloves are gloves and the one is not the other. Notice, too, that my thesis implicates me in the hypothesis that the pre-modern can communicate with the postmodern, which stands to reason if both are free from the kind of antagonism between faith and reason that grew up in and was so badly exacerbated by and in modernity. Notice, too, that in choosing Jacques Derrida as my representative of this new look at faith, I have chosen carefully—in class I try to stick to examples that work!—since not every philosopher who has taken a post-modern turn is interested in this dialogue with religion. A lot of them think that religion is one of the cardinal sins (the cardinal's sin!) and are still stuck in nineteenth-century reductionistic, conversation-stopping critiques of religion.

As always, we must be careful not to exaggerate. Jacques Derrida is worlds removed from Saint Augustine, literally and figuratively, as removed as a father of the church in late antiquity is from the father of twentieth-century "deconstruction," as removed as a Christian saint is from a Rive Gauche leftish Parisian intellectual and self-confessed atheist. So we must neither swallow this comparison whole nor dismiss it lightly. Remember that it is a mark of the postmodern to produce just such odd couples as this, like the buildings made of glass and steel that evoke the lines of Gothic cathedrals. Just so my Augustine/Derrida analogy. What matters in these edifices is whether they succeed, whether they produce sparks. Nothing guarantees in advance that they will or they will not; it depends upon how well it is done. I do not want this analogy to be completely implausible, nor do I want to make things too easy for myself. I want to preserve the tension between Augustine and Derrida and then harness its energy to launch us into the orbit of a postmodern theology, which is where I propose this ancient conversation between theology and philosophy now takes place.

Jacques Derrida was born in 1930 into a middle-class, French-speaking Jewish family in a suburb of Algiers. Algeria corresponds geographically to ancient Numidia, the land in which Augustine was born and where he served the church as a bishop in the North African church. Ancient Hippo is about a hundred miles from Algiers. He and Augustine are "compatriots," Derrida has quipped, and Derrida even lived for a while on a street called the Rue St. Augustin. Pre-war Algeria was a French colony where the dominant culture and language was what Derrida called "Christian Latin French." When during World War II the Jewish children were expelled from public school under order of the Vichy government, the orders came down in Latin, the same Latin that Derrida was taught in school and with which he would read Augustine. Like Augustine, he dreamed of leaving the provinces and going to the "metropolis" (Rome/Paris), to which they both traveled by sea, both getting seasick, both at the beginning of their careers in search of the "big apple." Like Augustine, he had to slip away from his mother, to whom he was greatly attached. Derrida was, he said, like Augustine, a man of tears, *filius istarum lacrymarum*, the son of his mother's tears, who wept and worried over her weepy son. When his mother (Georgette) lay dying in Nice, on the southern coast of France, he wrote a journal of the death watch he had to keep from afar due to his constant travels around the world, in a book he called *Circumfession*, which is a kind of postmodern counterpart to Augustine's *Confessions*. The latter, we recall, includes an account of Augustine's death watch at the side of Monica, in ancient Ostia, outside Rome, on the Mediterranean coast of Italy. As it happens, one of Derrida's journal entries is written from Santa Monica (California).

Derrida plays on this play of coincidences between him and Augustine in order to reconstruct the scene of the *Confessions*: Augustine/Jacques, Monica/Georgette, Rome/Paris, Ostia/Nice, and finally God/–? In the *Confessions*, Augustine is talking to God (not directly to us, by the way), but we are not sure to whom Derrida is speaking. He simply says "you," the way Augustine says "you" and where we know that Augustine means God. Does Derrida also mean God? Presumably not if he is an atheist, but you have to be careful with Derrida; you never know what he might have up his sleeve. Is he talking to himself? Not if he is writing, for there is (structurally) no private writing. His mother? Maybe, but we are all reading it and she never did, and the same goes for Geoffrey Bennington, to whom the text is officially directed if not finally addressed. To himself and others? Perhaps. Himself and his readers, his mother and God? That would be interesting. This play of coincidences, of the convergent circumstances of birth and life between himself and Augustine is, of course, also very serious, and religious people should be the last ones to downplay such play. If the play of chance is very important for Derrida, it is no less important for Augustine (*tolle, lege*), where it is interpreted as "grace"— please note: interpreted *as* grace, *as* a gift. What is taken *as* chance by Derrida is taken *as* grace by Augustine. So you see how important is this little hermeneutic "as," what a sea-change it can produce.

In one of the most interesting passages in this slightly enigmatic journal or book—it's a piece of avant-garde, experimental writing that ignores classical borders, which is another way it is postmodern—Derrida speaks of "my religion about which nobody understands anything...," an expression that is likely to get our attention coming as it does from a philosopher hitherto taken to be quite secular and one who had been sharply criticized by conservatives as a relativist and even a nihilist. "Any more than does my mother," he continues—she was afraid to ask him straight out whether he still believed in God, as she had taught him to do as a child, worrying over him like Monica over Augustine—"but she must have known that the constancy of God in my life is called by other names." God, the name of God, is not dismissed by Derrida, who would lack the authority to dismiss a word that belongs to a deeply inscribed vocabulary and goes back to time out of mind. It has an important function for Derrida, serving as it does to give life "constancy," serving we might say *as* life's constancy even though there are other names with which it is substitutable, or "translatable," names like "justice" or the "gift." For example, when someone says, "God is love," do they mean that "God" is one of the best names we have for love? Or is it the other way around (and this is what Augustine would have asked): Is "love" one of the best names we have for God? For Derrida there is an irresoluble slipping back and forth between these names and no place to stand that would give us the leverage to arrest this play. "So that I quite rightly pass for an atheist." Why not simply say, "I *am* an atheist"? Because that would be to arrest the play; it would have the self-assured ring of reductionism, the bluntness of nineteenth-century positivism, representing what Derrida once called "atheistic theology," by which he meant dogmatic atheism (he was using "theology" as a bad word, as a name for dogmatism). On the contrary, he thinks, what we call the "I" is implicated in a kind of conflict, of competing voices that give each other no rest, so that there is always an atheist within me who contests my professions of belief, just as there is always a believer within me who contests my professions of unbelief. That is why he says the name of God is the name of a secret that is withheld from him. Still, he "rightly passes" for an atheist—by the standards of the local pastor or rabbi. That is what others say about him, and that is right enough. But do not let saying that harden over into a dogma (not letting our beliefs and practices harden over into pure presence is a lot of what "deconstruction" means). Notice the Socratic ring to what Derrida is saying here and its similarity to Kierkegaard, when Kierkegaard says that he would never pretend to *be* a Christian, but at most professes trying to *become* one. Might it be that the best formula available to believers who are sensitive to the complex and multiple forces that are astir within us, as we all should be, is to claim that at most they "rightly pass" for a believer? Is this not an excellent formula for whatever we believe or do not believe?

In an equally surprising formulation, Derrida wonders "if I ought to tell them that I pray," adding, "for if you knew . . . my experience of prayers, you would know everything, you would tell me whom to address them to." He wonders, too, "if those reading me from up there see my tears, today, if they guess that my life was a long history of prayers, for these readers have understood everything, except that I have lived in prayer, tears." Like Augustine, he is a man of prayers and tears. But to whom is he praying? And for what does he weep? If he knew that, if someone could tell him all that, he would not need to pray. He prays because he does not know to whom to pray or if indeed there is someone there to receive his prayers. The very destitution of his prayer does not spell the end of prayer, but it is what drives his prayer. Theologians have sometimes asked if it is possible to pray to an unknown God. One theologian who has commented on the matter says that such an act would be an actual prayer to a virtual God— an actual and real prayer, directed to a God who is latent, potential.[9] Is there not something deep and rich about the poverty of Derrida's prayer? Do we not begin every prayer with a prayer for the prayer? Before we pray, do we not first say, "Lord, hear our prayers," and then we go on? Is there not a certain auto-effectiveness in prayer in virtue of which praying to be able to pray is already a prayer? Lord, we pray you, teach us to pray. Lord, I do believe, please help my unbelief. We pray from out of an inability to pray; we believe out of a backdrop of unbelief. Sometimes, in what Saint John of the Cross calls the "dark night of the soul," we continue to pray even though we are fully convinced that we no longer even believe in God. Then, at that precise moment when it is impossible to pray, prayer glows white hot.

Citing the *Confessions*, Derrida asks with Augustine, What do I love when I love my God and adds that he has been doing nothing all his life other than asking himself that question. When I love you, Augustine asks God, what is it that I love? The beautiful things in the world around me? The stars in the sky? No, no, Augustine answers on their behalf, for they all respond: God made us. Derrida shares Augustine's restless heart—*inquietum est cor nostrum*, our hearts are restless until they rest in you, Augustine had said—but Derrida cannot bring his restlessness to rest in a settled way upon a singular object of love, like Augustine's God. The function of the name of God for Derrida is not to effect the peacefulness of rest, but to stir up still more restless inquiry, because the constancy of God for him does not have one settled and definite name.

In another place Derrida introduces a distinction between what he calls the pure "messianic" and the concrete "messianisms." By the concrete messianisms he means first of all the *historical* "religions of the Book," Christianity, Judaism, and Islam, all of which have a messianic faith in the coming of a historical flesh and bones messiah and a coming messianic age. But he also means the *philosophical* messianisms—Hegel's, Marx's, and Heidegger's—where this same messianic faith is organized around a strictly philosophical eschatology, a philosophical faith and hope in a secular or purely historical dream, even, shall we say, a philosopher's prayer: for a classless society, for the time when we all become free, etc. From these historically concrete messianisms, Derrida differentiates the pure messianic, by which he means the pure form of hope and expectation, the very structure of the "to come" (*à venir*) which goes to the core of the very idea of the future (*l'avenir*), where the future is marked by its open-endedness and unforeseeableness. Of course, there is a relatively foreseeable future, what he calls the "future present," the future that we plan for and can reasonably expect to be the outcome of the present course of things. But that is not the "absolute future," a radically unforeseeable future where we hope with a hope against hope, as Saint Paul put it, in the coming of something, I do not know quite what, something for which the least bad names we have at present are names like "justice" or the "gift." This pure messianic cuts to the very core of our makeup, for our life consists in prayers and tears and we are always praying for the coming of justice, of the gift, of God, of something, I know not what, always asking, "What do I love when I love you, my God?"

How are we then to describe the difference between this classical theologian, Saint Augustine, a venerable father of the church, and Derrida, a contemporary philosopher who rightly passes for an atheist? Shall we say that Augustine has real faith and Derrida is in despair? That Augustine prays and Derrida is left without a prayer? Hardly, for Derrida, too, is a man of prayers and tears, with a faith that does not flag. No, the real difference that emerges is that when Augustine says "You," *(tu, te)*, he means the historically identifiable God of his forebearers, of the faith handed down over the ages from Abraham to the apostles and from the apostles to him and that he is handing on to us by writing this text. Further, when Augustine prays, he prays in concert with the community of faith, with the people of God, and he has available to him the words and the prayers and the stories that have constituted this people. In other words, the "you," the one to whom Augustine prays, has a proper, a determinate name, a name that is above all other names, at the sound of which every knee shall bend. So, too, Augustine's faith and hope and love have a determinate and specifiable destination (which is not to compromise its infinity). But the faith and love of Derrida, though real and resolute, can never settle into that kind of determinacy and nameability; they remain forever caught up in a kind of endless translatability, for he never knows the secret. The secret is, there is no secret, no privileged access to the secret, no knock-out punch that puts this play to rest. From Derrida's point of view, the determinate names at Augustine's disposal are so many ways to appropriate the secret, so many ways to determine the indeterminable, to name the unnameable, to arrest the play.

So there is something irreducibly religious and prayerful, faithful and hopeful about Derrida, every bit as much as there is about Augustine. Indeed, if I were not worried about starting up another turf war between philosophy and theology, I might even suggest, although it would be the height of imprudence to do so, that if indeed prayer is a kind of "wounded word," then Derrida's *Circumfession* is even *more* prayerful than Augustine's *Confessions*, because the words are more wounded, more cut—circum-cisional, circum-fessional—and hence even more confessional, more circumfessional, for he lacks the community and the assurances of Augustine. Remember that Augustine's *Confessions* were also a "confession" in the sense of *confiteor*, I confess or profess a particular faith, a determinate faith, whereas Derrida's is in a sense more purely confessional, confessing a faith in something that is simply withheld from him. So even though Derrida is an "atheist" and not a "theologian," there is something "religious" about him, in the sense of what he elsewhere called a "religion without religion."

The difference, then, between Augustine and Derrida, between a theologian who preceded modernity by many centuries and a philosopher in the postmodern mode, is not the difference between faith and faithlessness, or between hope and despair, or absolutism and relativism, but the difference between two faiths, two different kinds of faith—a determinate one, lodged in a concrete community of faith, and an indeterminate one, a little more lost and astray, but for all that no less deeply set and resolved, perhaps even, in its own way, a purer faith, a faith in faith itself. What we see transpiring in Augustine and Derrida is not a simple opposition of faith and disbelief, or hope and despair, but rather two different deployments of what the author of the Letter to the Hebrews called "the assurance (*hypostasis*, the stuff or substance) of things hoped for, the conviction of things not seen" (11:1), which is as good a characterization of faith as we are likely to find. It is not what we see that drives us on but what we do not, even as it is not the substantiality of what is all around us that awakens our hope but the insubstantiality, almost like a ghost, of what we hope for. That I take to be a principle of our lives and a principle of a postmodern faith, of a philosophical theology or of a theological philosophy (whichever version causes you less trouble), that is as old as the Scriptures.

E I G H T

I have spent all this time trying to get to just this point—let us call it a postmodern point, but that word does not matter much to me in the end. What matters is that if the account I have given is right, then the old boundaries and high walls that modernity tried to build around reason, science, and philosophy have come down. If that is so, then the language of faith has reacquired respectability, and if faith has been restored to its rightful place among the virtues, that gives theology, which turns on faith, a new opening. But by faith I do not mean faith as opposed to reason; if I am right, then that is a too simple opposition that I have tried to weaken and complicate without entirely discrediting it—there is nothing to be gained from erasing the distinction. By faith I mean faith as opposed to *cynicism*, to a cynical disbelief, a cynical refusal to believe that there is anything out there to command our respect, anything before whose majesty and beauty we are brought up short, any surpassing quality in things that leaves us wide-eyed and breathless. By faith I mean the feeling that wells up in us when we take our measure against some immeasurable immensity, like the feeling that stirs within us when we stand at the ocean's edge at midnight, alone except for the beating of the surf, watching a full moon illuminate a path that stretches from a quarter of a million miles away in space across the waves right up to our very feet.

Think of philosophers and theologians, then, as fellow sailors on that ocean, venturers and adventurers out over seventy thousand fathoms, old salts telling the rest of us stories while we, like youngsters with bulging eyes, take in every word.

Think of philosophy and theology as fellow travelers so that whatever theoretical distinctions or even oppositions there may be between the two, they are not opponents but companions on dangerous seas, attempting to make their way through life's riddles.

Think of philosophy and theology as different moments in a common passion, different voices in a common song we sing, different ways to respond to the common darkness by which we are all enveloped, fellow pilgrims on a path we all must follow, where we all—both philosophers and theologians, both scientists and poets—have to concede we are a little lost, which is really the only way to begin a search.

Think of philosophy and theology as companion planets orbiting around a common center, held in the gravitational pull of an absolute secret that sits in the middle while they trace concentric circles around a central mystery.

In sum, and I now come to my final thesis (I promise): my own hypothesis is that philosophy and theology are different but companion ways to nurture what I will call the *passion of life*. My dominant interest, my preoccupying passion, lies in what gives life its passion, what lifts us up above the humdrum drift of indifference and mediocrity and gives us something surpassing to love beyond ourselves, something surpassing to seek beyond the empty consumerism of wandering through shopping malls in an endless search for more possessions. One of the important things to emerge from the study of our postmodern odd couple, Augustine/Derrida, is the centrality of that question, "What do I love when I love my God?"

What I love about that question is that it assumes that loving God is everything and then wants to know in just what that love consists, which is why it can be formulated by Augustine in a completely theological context and then, some sixteen centuries later, can be repeated and recontextualized by Derrida in his own highly unorthodox philosophical way. That is because the question cuts to the quick and goes all the way down; it is in an important sense *the* question, the one and overarching question we have to pose, the question of what we love, of what gives life passion—if anything does. The opposite of loving God is cynicism, loving nothing, which translates into loving ourselves in an unenlightened way. I am not against loving oneself; if you do not love yourself, nothing will matter to you because you do not think yourself worth loving. I *am* against loving oneself in a selfish and self-acquisitive way at the expense of loving others and loving God.

What interests me more than Derrida interests me and more than Augustine interests me is how Derrida and Augustine communicate with each other across an abyss, how something similar is going on *between* this theologian and this philosopher, *across* the chasm that separates Augustine's *Confessions* and Derrida's *Circumfession*. What is that? It is a prayer. In each a prayer is sent up into the night destined we know not where, although we have different views corresponding to our several faiths. And a tear. In each a tear falls for something coming, we know not what, something that will transform us, for which we lack the name, for which all present names are lacking. Each is praying and weeping over some elusive and unknown messianic age.

On the view that I take, we are all praying and weeping over our existence, over what gives our lives intensity, urgency, depth, passion, the lack of which results in the superficial life. While I clearly have Derrida and Augustine in mind when I say this, I am also making use of theologian Paul Tillich, for whom the very meaning of God is to be the depth and mystery of our being. This matter of the passion of life is why I turn to philosophy and to theology, or rather why they have overtaken and overturned me. I find myself running a kind of shuttle back and forth between the two, dashing from one to the other like a man trying to hold down two different jobs in two different parts of towns. It is not as though I have a choice in the matter. For I have been seduced by them, induced, lured, fetched from afar, wrenched from out of my everyday life, and hauled into their chambers where I am made to answer for myself.

I have been—and perhaps this is the best figure of all—wounded by their words, the way one speaks of being wounded by love's arrow. Philosophy and theology are for wounded souls. Indeed those of us who take up the study of any of the humanities, of language and literature, history and art, philosophy and theology, or any of the natural sciences, have been pierced to the heart by something precious, beautiful, deep, and enigmatic that leaves us reeling. We know that the doctors are not telling us everything, that the wound will not heal, that we are not going to recover. We have suffered a blow that has destroyed our equilibrium; we have been shaken by a provocation, by something that has left us breathless, pursued by questions that we cannot still. We have been visited by some affliction that results in tremors (that is how it "presents itself," as the medical textbooks say), but also has this other oddity about it—this disorder induces an affection for our affliction, so that the patients have no wish to be healed, to close this wound over, to arrest these tremors. For we live and breathe in the tremulousness of our lives, exposed to the questionability of things, made vulnerable to love's wounds, visited in the night by questions of elemental power, shaken to the core by voices that will not be stilled.

We are nourished by the depths that spread out before us, luring us on like sirens. Life, we think, is like a star that shines all the more brilliantly the darker the night. It is the darkness that gives things their depth, and we are prepared to give the darkness its due, not because we are obscurantists but because we love the brightness of the stars. The dark ring of ambiguity around life is a crucial ingredient in its richness; it is not something to be dispersed so that we can lead unambiguous lives. On the contrary, the ambiguity provokes interpretation, like a classic text that has invited centuries of commentary, forcing us to come to grips with depths that elude our grip, that will not succumb to our grip. In responding to this provocation, in offering such interpretations as seem plausible, we reach a certain self-understanding, even if that is the understanding that we can never quite understand who we are and that there is no one final interpretation. The opposite of all this, the result of turning our backs on the enigma of our lives and embracing unqualified and unambiguous clarity, is the superficial life, a life made artificially easy by facile answers and too easy acquisitions.

That is why I turn repeatedly to the *Confessions* of Saint Augustine, that great document in the history of literature, philosophy, and theology (to the consternation of all modernist divisions of labor, it is all three at once!), where Augustine described these tremors in the very first chapter of his book: *inquietum est cor nostrum*. We are all suffering from a congenital heart condition, the "dis-ease" of a restless heart, a heart made restless by the search for something I know not what, for something whose name is above every other name, or for something whose name is in principle withheld. Either way, the only way to proceed is with a certain faith, for this faith is faith in life itself. In the end, the several faiths are each a faith in existence itself, in the very stuff of life itself, in the force that surges through our lives and gives each day its spark, its joy, which is also why we suffer so badly when life goes wrong. Our misery is made all the more miserable because it is the corruption of something splendid, which is why the sacred scriptures of every religion enjoin us to lift up the neediest and most helpless of God's children. Good, good, good, good, good—very good, said Elohim. Yes, yes, again, I say yes, said Molly Bloom.[10] We have tasted the wormwood, the bitterness of life, but we still say yes. Come, Lord Jesus. "*Viens, oui, oui,*" says Derrida.

When you read the *Confessions* you should approach it as if you had stumbled upon a man at prayer, for that is just what has happened. Augustine's back is turned to us and he is turned to God, to "you" (*tu*), while we are like intruders on the scene. When Saint Augustine confessed himself "before God" (*coram deo*), he also found himself confessing face to face with himself. One of the things we mean by God is that power or principle or person that opens up the secret or private chambers of the "self." It was in this moment of the clear/obscure, in the deepest moments of a self-meditation that was also at the same time a meditation upon and before God, that Augustine was led to write, *quaestio mihi factus sum,* I have been made a question to myself. When he lived a superficial life, he knew exactly what he wanted and who he was, or thought he was—an ambitious orator, a rising star in the world of Roman public life, a lover of love's pleasures— but when he was brought up short before God, his life in the world opened up in an abyss of endless questionability. Who or what is this God, this power of infinity, this depth of being, before whom he has been called, and who am I who stand before God? What do I love when I love this God, he asked. He called all this his "confessions," and Derrida added his "circumfessions," meaning his wounds. But these are the strangest sort of wounds, made up of cuts that cut us loose from the vanities of the superficial life and bring us face to face with the complexity and perplexity of life, with life's darkest center. That perplexity is what gives life beauty and depth, passion and power, even while it decenters us, knocks us off our pins, robs us of the ease with which we negotiate the rapids of everyday life, divesting us of the sense that we have everything in control.

If you take a long enough look, beyond the debates that divide philosophy and theology, over the walls that they have built to keep each other out or beyond the wars to subordinate one to the other, you find a common sense of awe, a common gasp of surprise or astonishment, like looking out at the endless sprawl of stars across the evening sky or upon the waves of a midnight sea.

Does anyone know we are here? Nietzsche asked, and he asked this for us all.

In all this lies the passion.

NOTES

1. That is the basis of the distinction made by Paul Tillich between "correlational" and "non-correlational" theologies. Correlational theologies seek to establish the relation or rapport between the being of God and human being, where God is always God-for-us and we are always we-for-God; where the Word of God answers a question that the theologian poses in the midst of the present situation and theology undergoes constant reformulation under changing needs and new questions. "Non-correlational" theologies emphasize the transcendence and total otherness of God and the timeless shock that the Word of God delivers to worldly institutions and to the worldliness of philosophy. In correlational theology we must prepare the conditions to receive the Word, whereas non-correlational is "kerygmatic," like the theology of Karl Barth, emphasizing that the Word has been unconditionally "proclaimed," whether we are ready or not, whether we like it or not.

2. Indeed, religious ideas sink down so far into the roots of a culture that they persist even after a person or a group or a culture disavows the religious faith that spawned these thoughts to begin with. That is what is behind much of the "church and state" debates we have today. What we take to be public consensus and secular common sense, that each individual has inalienable rights, are ideas with biblical roots held in the secrecy of our hearts, e.g., that God knows and loves each one of us. That is an idea that holds on even if faith in God does not.

3. A *polis* was an autonomous Greek city with the political status of a sovereign state. Each city had its characteristic culture, its patron gods, its model form of life and model virtues—in Sparta, courage; in Athens, wisdom—that formed each citizen like a motherly womb.

4. See Jacob Needleman, *The American Soul: Rediscovering the Wisdom of the Founders* (New York: Tarcher Books, 2003).

5. When historians looked around to determine where to point the finger for this disaster even Thomas Aquinas, who gave reason its own play, became suspect. But if the idea was to pinpoint the precise moment when philosophy, and hence reason, began to twist free from theology, John Duns Scotus (d. 1308), the great Franciscan master, is a still more interesting suspect. That is because Scotus was the first philosopher to hold that both God and creatures come "under" the common idea of "being," which is at root the same sort of thinking that led Descartes to say that both God and creatures both come "under" the principle of causality. That implies a certain shrinking down of God to fit under the canopy of reason and hence the subordination of theology to the jurisdiction of philosophy. Thomas Aquinas, however, was a deeply theological thinker from this point of view because he held that compared to the very being of God, the idea of being in general was just an abstraction.

6. Blaise Pascal, *Pensées*, trans. A. J. Krailsheimer (Baltimore: Penguin Books, 1995).

7. Rudolph Bultmann, *Jesus Christ and Mythology* (New York: Scribners, 1958), 15.

8. James Joyce, *Finnegans Wake* (London: Faber & Faber, 1960), 118.

9. Jean-Luis Chrétien, "The Wounded Word: The Phenomenology of Prayer," trans. Jeffrey Kosky in *Phenomenology and the "Theological Turn": The French Debate* (New York: Fordham University Press, 2001).

10. James Joyce, *Ulysses,* ed. Hans Walter Gambler (New York: Vintage Books, 1986), 643–644.

APPENDIX

Cast of Characters in Chronological Order

Socrates (469–399 BCE), Plato's teacher and inspiration, said that "the unexamined life is not worth living" (Plato, *Apology*, 42a). He left no writings behind and is best known to us from the early dialogues of Plato—see Plato, *The Last Days of Socrates*, ed. Harold Tarrant, trans. Hugh Tredennick (New York: Penguin, 1993), and Xenophon, *Conversations of Socrates*, trans. Robin H. Waterfield and Hugh Tredennick (New York: Penguin, 1990). See also Aristophanes, *Clouds*, trans. Peter Meineck (Indianapolis: Hackett Pub. Co., 2000).

Plato (427–337 BCE) put Western philosophy on the map; his works—the *Republic* is the most famous—are the inescapable frame of reference for all subsequent philosophers. See *Plato: The Collected Dialogues*, ed. Edith Hamilton and Huntington Cairns (Princeton: Bollingen Series, 1961). Of the countless introductions available, G. M. Grube, *Plato* (reissue, Boston: Beacon Press, 2000), is clear and reliable.

Aristotle (384–322 BCE), with Plato the cofounder of Western philosophy, a student of Plato who struck out in a different direction. See *The Basic Works of Aristotle*, ed. Richard McKeon (repr., New York: The Modern Library, 2001). Marjorie Grene, *A Portrait of Aristotle* (repr. South Bend: St. Augustine's Press, 1998), is an excellent place to start.

Saint Paul is, well, Saint Paul. On the matter of his attitude to philosophy, see Stanislas Breton, *The Word and the Cross*, trans. Jacquelyn Porter (New York: Fordham Univ. Press, 2002).

Saint Augustine (354–430), the greatest of the early fathers of the Christian Church. He drew upon the works of Plato and the Neoplatonic philosophers, and is best known for *Confessions*, trans. F. J. Sheed (Indianapolis: Hackett Pub. Co., 1970)—I used Books I and X in particular—and *The City of God*, trans. Henry Bettenson (repr. Baltimore: Penguin Books, 2003). His "If I doubt, I am" argument can be found in *The City of God*, Book XI, chap. 26. The best general introduction I know is Garry Wills, *Saint Augustine* (New York: Penguin, 1999). I also recommend Paul Tillich's essay on the difference between Saint Augustine and Saint Thomas Aquinas, "Two Theories of the Philosophy of Religion," in *Theology of Culture*, pp. 10-29. (See Paul Tillich below.)

Saint Anselm (1033–1109) proposed the famous "ontological argument" in his *Proslogian*, but he is also known for the theory of penal substitution in *Why God Became Man*. See *Anselm of Canterbury: The Major Works*, ed. Brian Davies and G. R. Evans (Oxford: Oxford Univ. Press, 1998).

Moses Maimonides (Moses ben Maimon, 1135–1204) was the greatest of the medieval Jewish philosophical theologians who, like Aquinas (Aquinas often cited Maimonides), relied upon Aristotle to interpret the Scriptures. His most famous work is *A Guide for the Perplexed*, trans. M. Friedlander (New York: Dover Books, 1904, 1956). In the Islamic world the dominant philosophical figures were **Avicenna** (Ibn-Sina, 980–1037) and **Averroes** (Ibn Roschd, 1126–1198). For the history of Islam and its influence on medieval Europe, see the works of William Montgomery Watt.

Saint Thomas Aquinas (1225–1274), the greatest of the theologians of the High Middle Ages and of the Roman Catholic tradition, drew upon the Latin translations of Aristotle in his classic *Summa Theologica*, 5 vol., trans. Fathers of the English Dominican Province (Christian Classics, 1981). For the remark about not detracting from God's creation, see his other major work, *Summa Contra Gentiles*, ed. Vernon Bourke (South Bend: Univ. of Notre Dame Press, 1976), Book III, chap. 69. The best general commentary may well be Etienne Gilson, *The Christian Philosophy of Saint Thomas Aquinas*, trans. I. T. Shook (South Bend: Univ. of Notre Dame Press, 1994).

Galileo Galilei (1564–1642) is one of the founders of modern science. He built the first telescopes that supported the Copernican theory but was silenced by the Church in a famous trial. His story has recently received a personal twist with the publication of Dava Sobel, *Galileo's Daughter: A Historical Memoir of Science, Faith, and Love* (Baltimore: Penguin, 2000).

René Descartes (1596–1650) transformed the history of Western philosophy with his 1641 *Meditations on First Philosophy*, trans. Donald Cress (Indianapolis: Hackett Publishing Co, 1993), and influenced in particular **Gottfried Wilhelm von Leibniz** (1646–1716), a brilliant mathematician and logician as well as a philosopher, and **Benedict de Spinoza,** a Jewish freethinker who was expelled from the synagogue for his unorthodox idea of *deus sive natura* ("God or nature").

Immanuel Kant (1720–1804), along with Hegel the greatest of all the German philosophers and the high point of Enlightenment thought, is best known for the *Critique of Pure Reason*, ed. Paul Guyer and Allen Wood (Cambridge: Cambridge Univ. Press, 1998), the first of a famous trilogy of *"Critiques."* His mains works on religion are found in *Religion and Rational Theology*, ed. Allen Wood (Cambridge: Cambridge Univ. Press, 1996). "What is Enlightenment?" is online at http://www.english.upenn.edu/~mgamer/Etexts/kant.html.

Georg Friedrich Wilhelm Hegel (1770–1831) is the high point of "German Idealism," and a defining point for all continental philosophy thereafter. His single most important book is *Phenomenology of Spirit*, trans. A. V. Miller (Oxford: Oxford Univ. Press, 1977). My account was primarily drawn from *Lectures on the Philosophy of Religion*, ed. Peter C. Hodgson (Berkeley: Univ. of California Press, 1988), 391–489.

Gotthold Ephraim Lessing (1729–1781) composed *Nathan the Wise* (1799), claiming the three great monotheistic religions boil down to a common ethic. See *Nathan the Wise, Minna Von Barnhelm, and Other Plays and Writings* (New York: Continuum, 1991).

Friedrich Schleiermacher (1768–1834) is a giant in modern liberal Protestant theology and the author of one of its most famous definitions of religion (a feeling of absolute dependence). See *On Religion: Speeches to its Cultured Despisers*, trans. John Oman (New York: Harper Torch Books, 1958).

Søren Kierkegaard (1813–1855), the father of "existentialism" and an important source for the religious version of "postmodernism," is most famous for *Fear and Trembling*, ed. and trans. Howard and Edna Hong (Princeton: Princeton

Univ. Press, 1983), and *Concluding Unscientific Postscript to "Philosophical Fragments,"* ed. and trans. Howard and Edna Hong (Princeton: Princeton Univ. Press, 1992). He discusses Socrates frequently, but I was citing *The Moment and Late Writings*, ed. and trans. Howard and Edna Hong (Princeton: Princeton Univ. Press, 1998), 340–43.

Friedrich Nietzsche (1844–1900), well known for his famous assertion that "God is dead," is the most important nineteenth-century background figure for the anti-theological side of postmodern thought. See *Beyond Good and Evil,* trans. R. J. Hollingdale (reissue, New York: Penguin Books, 2003), and *Twilight of the Idols* and *The Anti-Christ,* trans. R. J. Hollingdale (New York: Penguin Books, 1969). The opening quotation about the little star is found in "On Truth and Lies in a Nonmoral Sense," in *Philosophy and Truth: Selections from Nietzsche's Notebooks of the Early 1870s,* ed. and trans. Daniel Breazeale (Atlantic Highlands, N.J.: Humanities Press International, 1979), 79.

Alfred North Whitehead (1861–1947), co-author of *Principia Mathematica* with Bertrand Russell in 1910–1913 (Cambridge: Cambridge Univ. Press, 1962), which laid the foundation of modern logic, gave the 1927–1928 Gifford lectures published as *Process and Reality,* Corrected Edition, ed. David Ray Griffin and Donald Shelburne (New York: Free Press, 1958), which laid the foundation of "process theology." His most famous disciple was Charles Hartshorne. This work is continued today by philosophical theologians like John Cobb, Robert Neville, and David Ray Griffin.

Karl Barth (1886–1968), the father of modern neo-orthodoxy, shocked the liberal theological establishment in 1919 with the first edition of his *Commentary on the Letter to the Romans,* trans. Edwin C. Hoskyns from the 6th German ed.

(Oxford: Oxford Univ. Press, 1933). He went on to compose the monumental (4 vol. but 13 books) *Church Dogmatics* [1936–75], 2nd ed., ed. and trans. G. W. Bromiley and Thomas F. Torrance (paperback repr., Edinburgh: T. & T. Clark, 1975–77, 2004). We referred to his *Anselm: Fides Quaerens Intellectum*, trans. of 2nd ed., ed. Ian W. Robertson (London: SCM Press, 1960).

Paul Tillich (1886–1965), one of the great progressive theologians of the twentieth century, is the author of *Systematic Theology*, 3 vols. (Chicago: Univ. of Chicago, 1951–63). Tillich explains the distinction between the "correlational" method he follows and the "non-correlational" methods of someone like Barth in vol. I, pp. 59–66. See also his *Theology of Culture* (New York: Oxford Univ. Press, 1964).

Martin Heidegger (1889–1976), the most important of all the twentieth-century Continental philosophers, associated with both existentialism and postmodernism, is most famous for his 1927 classic *Being and Time*, trans. John Macquarrie and Edward Robinson (New York: Harper & Row, 1962), which laid the basis of contemporary hermeneutics. His remarks about "Christian philosophy" can be found in *An Introduction to Metaphysics*, trans. Ralph Mannheim (New Haven: Yale Univ. Press, 1959), 6–7, 142–43. His *The Principle of Reason*, trans. Reginald Lilly (Bloomington: Indiana Univ. Press, 1991), is a brilliant sketch of the emergence of the "modern" and its idea of "reason."

Ludwig Wittgenstein (1889–1951) is a Viennese-born philosopher who dominated the Anglo-American scene of "analytic philosophy" the way Heidegger dominates the scene of "Continental philosophy." His most important books are his 1921 *Tractatus Logico-Philosophicus*, trans. D. F. Pears and B. F. McGuinness (London: Routledge, 1974), on the pure logical structure of language, and his 1953 *Philosophical Investigations*, 2nd ed., trans. G. E. M. Anscombe (Oxford: Blackwell, 1998), on the subtleties of ordinary language. See his *Lectures and Conversations on Aesthetics, Psychology, Religious Belief*, ed. Cyril Barrett (Oxford: Blackwell, 1966). D. Z. Phillips is the leading Wittgensteinian philosopher of religion today.

Thomas Kuhn (1922–1996) changed the course of American philosophy of science with his 1962 publication *The Structure of Scientific Revolutions*, 2nd ed. (Chicago: Univ. of Chicago Press, 1986). This book grew out of a previous book on Copernicus, *The Copernican Revolution: Planetary Astronomy in the Development of Western Thought* (Cambridge: Harvard Univ. Press, 1957), where you will find an excellent history of the birth of modern science. His work—along with that of Wittgenstein and Heidegger—was taken up by "post-analytic" thinkers like Richard Rorty, whose *Philosophy and the Mirror of Nature* (Princeton: Princeton Univ. Press, 1981) made postmodern ideas a topic of discussion in Anglo-American thought.

Jean-François Lyotard (1924–1998), one of the foremost exponents of postmodern theories of art, ethics, and knowledge, established the word "postmodern" in the contemporary vocabulary in 1979 with his *The Postmodern Condition: A Report on Knowledge*, trans. Geoff Bennington and Brian Massumi (Minneapolis: Univ. of Minnesota Press, 1984). He was also writing about Augustine's *Confessions* at the time of his death: *The Confession of Augustine*, trans. Richard Beardsworth (Stanford: Stanford Univ. Press, 2000).

Jacques Derrida (1930–2004), who introduced the word "deconstruction," is the author of numerous books, but we have concentrated on the discussion of Saint Augustine in "Circumfession: Fifty-nine Periods and Periphrases" in

Geoffrey Bennington and Jacques Derrida, *Jacques Derrida* (Chicago: Univ. of Chicago Press, 1993), especially pp. 138–40, 154–55, 187–88. The analysis of Derrida by Bennington, also found in that book, is highly recommended. On the pure "messianic" see *Specters of Marx*, trans. Peggy Kamuf (New York: Routledge, 1994). For more about Derrida and Augustine, see *Augustine and Postmodernism: Confessions and Circumfession*, ed. John D. Caputo and Michael Scanlon (Bloomington: Indiana Univ. Press, 2005).

Jean-Luc Marion (1946–) is the leading figure in the revival in the philosophy of religion in France and the United States; his best known book is *God Without Being*, trans. Thomas Carlson (Chicago: Univ. of Chicago Press, 1991), but he is also a leading Descartes scholar. The basis of my discussion of the *causa sui* is found in *On Descartes' Metaphysical Prism*, trans. Jeffrey Kosky (Chicago: Univ. of Chicago Press, 1999), 244–61.

CPSIA information can be obtained at www.ICGtesting.com
Printed in the USA
LVOW060219100212

267979LV00001B/67/P